The
Ulster
Fry

The Ulster Fry

THE NEWS
AS IT SHOULD BE

BLACKSTAFF PRESS
BELFAST

First published in 2016 by
Blackstaff Press
4D Weavers Court
Linfield Road
Belfast BT12 5GH

Designed by Lisa Dynan
Printed in Northern Ireland by W&G Baird

ISBN 978 0 85640 987 5

www.blackstaffpress.com
www.theulsterfry.com

Contents

Thanks   6

Introduction   7

Spring   8

Summer   38

Autumn   68

Winter   98

Index   128

Thanks

Thanks to all our readers for
the likes, shares and comments
that make running this site such
good craic. Keep 'er lit.

Introduction

Online comedy in this neck of the woods has always been as parochial and fragmented as the place itself. Sites like The Portadown News, Pure Derry, CSI Plumbridge and Tyrone Tribulations, have all provided wit and (occasionally) wisdom from scattered corners of the Province, but never has one publication spoken for us all – cos we don't agree on stuff, apparently.

In spring 2014 Ciaran 'Seamus' Murray, the (then) anonymous rogue reporter responsible for Pure Derry contacted the fictional professor behind the CSI Plumbridge and Jackie Fullerton pages, Ivan 'Billy' Minnis, to change all that. The pair agreed to launch a new, Northern Ireland-wide satirical page and immediately set about doing nothing for six months.

Eventually, however, they got around to launching The Ulster Fry in December 2014, and got to work capturing the true essence of Northern Ireland life by making stuff up whilst sitting on the bus or the toilet at work. Two years, five million reads, three elections, one Brexit and a crisp sandwich cafe later, this book is the result.

We rarely talk about our process, or the 'why' (mostly cos it's kinda dull and pretentious) but The Ulster Fry is really about celebrating what unites us, not what divides us. As we hope we've shown this last lock of years, there's much more of it than people would have you believe.

Huge thanks are due to occasional contributors and head-melters such as Stephen, Aine, Shanks, John B, James N and Gaz, and to the bazillion Loyal and Republican readers around the world who've liked, shared and commented on the stories over the past couple of years.

In particular to our long suffering partners who've had to listen to us talk shite and put up with us ignoring them while we make stuff up on the laptops.

Welcome to
St Bigots
School For Themuns

BBC
TOPLESS SPIDE FORECAST
ULSTER BRACES ITSELF FOR SUNSHINE

14:00
WEDNESDAY

ÙN

ÙN

ÙN

$$\frac{ab - x \cap y = r + \Omega x - a}{3z}$$

yer ma

= quare
stretch in
the evening

The Ulster Fry

MUCKERS

POOTERS

The Ulster Fry

Spring

'I can now definitively say that the exact location of the first quare stretch in the evening is 5.33 p.m. on 3 March, in a field just outside Cookstown.'

Couple to stare at takeaway menu for ages before ordering same shite as usual

With the latest weather forecast indicating it would 'founder ye', The Ulster Fry has learned that one local couple intends to spend their Saturday evening agonising over a takeaway menu for ages – before ordering the same shite they always get.

The couple, who claim they 'fancy a wee change tonight', plan on sifting through the huge pile of takeaway menus on the hall telephone table to find one that is still in business – before

indecisively passing it back and forth between themselves for the entire duration of ITV dating show *Take Me Out.*

'Thon honey-chilli chicken dish looks nice,' they mused, 'but we'll be raging with ourselves if it's rotten. What about the black bean sauce? Oh aye, that gives you heartburn. Wonder what that Kung-Po Chicken is like? Always wanted to try that – but then again, I might not like it.'

'Feck it, will we just get the

usual?' they asked, before ordering the same thing they got last week, and the week before, off the top of their heads, without actually needing to see it written down.

'Quare stretch in the evenings,' confirms Professor Stephen Hawking

World-renowned scientist Stephen Hawking has confirmed that there is indeed a 'quare stretch in the evenings' as of today.

Best known for his role in the movie *The Theory of Everything*, Professor Hawking told fellow scientists that he had been studying the 'stretch in the evening' phenomenon for some time, in the hope of finding an exact point when the word 'quare' could be added to the statement.

'For so long mankind has been pondering the nature of the

universe,' the former Simpsons star told a hushed audience, 'struggling to find seasonal small talk about the weather to pass ourselves with work colleagues.'

Continuing in that robot voice he has, Professor Hawking said that he had dedicated his life to the study of quarks, 'only to realise late in my career that it is "quare" that matters. I can now definitively say that the exact location of the first quare stretch in the evening is 5.33 p.m. on 18 February in a field just outside Cookstown.'

Fellow scientists the world over have hailed the professor's work. 'This is revolutionary work,' said Harvard University's Dr Hank Wankelfecker. 'He must be a shoo-in for a Nobel Prize for something, or maybe even a MOBO award.'

Sir Stephen will publish his latest findings in a new work – *A Brief History of Shite I Left Out of that Other Book* – before beginning a new research project.

'I'm setting out to discover when "wile close" becomes "swelterin", so I am,' he told us.

❝ I can now definitively say that the exact location of the first quare stretch in the evening is 5.33 p.m. on 18 Februry in a field just outside Cookstown, ❞ states Professor Hawking.

Trendy Cathedral Quarter pub set to open world's first 'Beard Garden'

With the summer fast approaching, Belfast's hipster-led social scene is set to grow even bigger – with the opening of the world's first 'Beard Garden'. Whilst the new outdoor area is still under construction, local pub tycoon and hotelier Will Ballsy told us that his new 'Beard Garden' will celebrate the 'hairy best of Belfast' with a 'wee bit of humour and sophistication'.

'If you look at London, Berlin and New York, it's clear that innovative and quirky nightlife ideas are leading the way in how modern consumers socialise. So as we sought to expand our commercial activities in 2015, we looked at what made Belfast unique.'

'The trends that came up again and again in our research were our ability to laugh at ourselves, our famous sense of humour and the sheer quantity of big massive f**k-off beards!'

Opening soon in the former waste ground between The National and The Spaniard, 'Sparta' will be a contemporary outdoor haven for Belfast's bearded socialites. As expected, it will have a strict 'beard only' dress-code policy, and serve a huge selection of niche craft and imported beers in oddly designed bottles and ridiculously shaped pint glasses.

'Girls will be allowed in too of course!' laughed Ballsy. 'But only if they have a bearded friend.' Inspired by the infamous antics of bearded, super-rich and promiscuous American playboy, Dan Bilzerian, Ballsy told us that Sparta's female admission policy would allow 'one bearded man to come with several women per night'.

'In fact bouncer training has already begun,' he continued. 'If a clean-shaven man tries to evade our security team, our bouncers will simply dropkick him out the door again, whilst politely reminding him – "This Is Sparta"!'

The news has already divided local opinion with people damning it as a 'blatant publicity stunt' and 'another f**king hipster cash in.' However not all punters agreed. 'I don't actually get it,' admitted Bristle McKeever, a twenty-four year-old amateur Googler from Stranmillis. 'Aren't they just copying the Dirty Onion?'

> ❝ The Beard Garden will celebrate the hairy best of Belfast with humour and sophistication, ❞ said pub tycoon Will Ballsy.

Petrol stations brace themselves for a busy Mother's Day

The chairman of the Northern Ireland Association of Petrol Stations has revealed that their forecourts and garage shops are 'fully stocked and loaded' tonight ahead of tomorrow's Mother's Day celebrations.

'We've got fresh flowers out the front in a rake of black buckets,' revealed Duncan Richtee, 'a heap of crap cards over beside the crisps there … plus a whole clatter of fancy chocolates, like Milk Tray, Black Magic and 12-packs of Kit Kats.'

'Mammies will be well looked after the marra, bai!' he added.

Mother's Day – an annual tribute to women who've given birth – is traditionally remembered by their male offspring whilst hungover sometime tomorrow morning, leading to a hasty cross-country exodus to spoil their beloved mammy with the finest goods that wherever the hell is still open is selling.

'I got spoilt rotten last year,' revealed local mammy Pamela Rusk. 'Our Lisa and Donna took me out for a swanky brunch at the Killyrea Hotel, and later that afternoon our Liam landed in with a lovely bag of fresh-picked spuds and twenty-four free-range eggs. Ach, sure, they shouldn't have bothered.'

Her neighbour Tammy Dodger agreed. 'Our John came in last year and said "Mammy, you're always saying you want to Take a Break. So I got you that, plus some other magazines you'll like, like *Woman's Own*, *Good Housekeeping* and *Ulster Tatler*.

'Plus the big dote brought me breakfast in bed,' she continued. 'I got jambons, sausage rolls, chicken vol-au-vents and a Cornish pasty. He even brought me a sachet of brown sauce.'

Given that most men will be up all night skulling cans of beer and shouting at the TV during the Conor McGregor fight, experts at the Larne School of Economics today predicted that 74 per cent of mammies will receive Easter Eggs tomorrow for Mother's Day.

Ulsterbus hijacker 'just trying to avoid wife', say police

A 45-year-old man who hijacked the 212 Maiden City Flyer from Derry to Belfast today was 'in wile bother with his missus' according to our sources in the PSNI.

In a virtual mirror image of the more widely reported EgyptAir hijacking, unemployed male impersonator Damien Scunder boarded the bus at the Claudy stop and demanded to be taken to Libya, telling the driver that he was wearing a suicide vest packed with explosives.

Passengers immediately began using the somewhat erratic wi-fi service on the Goldliner coach to report on the developments.

'This boy's going clean buck mental,' tweeted @Derry_girl48. 'He says he's been on the lash since Good Friday and his wife's going to kill him #AnotherGoldlinerHijack.'

It appears the driver told Mr Scunder that Libya was not on his route and that he could only take him as far as the Europa Bus Centre, but that if he wanted he could drop him off at Castledawson and he could try to get a connection to the airport. However, once there, the bus was immediately surrounded by the PSNI, who by coincidence were parked outside the big branch of KFC, again.

'Peelers all over,' tweeted passenger @yermaskeks. 'Some of them have even dropped their chips. #BusHijackKFC.'

A tense stand-off followed, during which the hijacker made a series of demands including the immediate handover of a Bargain Bucket with extra beans and a signed photo of Pamela Ballantine, before officers finally brought the crisis to an end by boarding the bus and surrounding him.

At this point it became clear that Mr Scunder was not, in fact, a hijacker. His 'suicide vest' was actually a string vest and he didn't really want to be taken to Libya, he wanted to go to Limavady.

Everyone on the bus has been arrested and charged with wasting police time.

'Peelers all over,' tweeted passenger @yermaskeks. 'Some of them have even dropped their chips. #BusHijackKFC.'

'What's wrong with having NO insurance?', asks a disgruntled Ian Paisley Jr

First Minister Arlene Foster was forced to call an emergency news conference today after it emerged that North Antrim MP Ian Paisley Jr had been convicted of driving with no insurance.

'Driving with No insurance is a key part of DUP policy,' Mrs Foster told reporters. 'We have to ensure that the word no is used as often as possible. We also have no tax and no MOT.'

Mr Paisley then interrupted his leader, took the microphone and burst into operatic song …

'No Compare! No Compare!
Use your vote, to save us dopes
At No Compare
Unless our vote gets bigger, you'll get a Shinner,
Everyone must vote for No Compare
No Compare! No Compare!
Use your senses and claim expenses

At No Compare
Even if you're not Free P,
You too can vote for DUP,
Switch your vote to No Compare.'

When then asked if the DUP policy to say 'No' to stuff all the time was part of her leadership strategy, Mrs Foster replied, 'NEVER!'

The news conference came to an abrupt end when someone called a taxi for The Ulster Fry.

> ❝ Driving with No insurance is a key part of DUP policy. We have to ensure that the word no is used as often as possible. We also have no tax and no MOT, ❞ said Arlene Foster.

nocompare.com

UN organises peacekeeping force of mammies for Holylands

With the Holylands area of Belfast once again awash with St Patrick's Day vomit, we can reveal that the United Nations is to send in a Peacekeeping Force of Tyrone Mammies in an attempt to defuse tensions.

The students began their annual celebration of the apostle of Ireland late last night, gathering in the streets to vandalise cars and fight each other in a traditional and inclusive manner, before complaining that the police were spoiling 'the craic'. The 'party atmosphere' has continued this morning.

'Sure it's mighty craic altogether,' we were told by twenty-year-old Ben Burb, a student of Anti-Social Behaviour at Queen's, as he squatted in his neighbour's garden having a shit. 'It's typical of the police to wade in and ruin it.'

His girlfriend Donna Managh, who studies shoes at the University of Ulster, complained that students were getting a bad name. 'It's all a bit of harmless fun,' she told us. 'We weren't doing anyone any harm and sure we'll all bunch up to fix the cars and windows we broke. As soon as our next student loan comes in,' she added.

However police are now confident the rest of St Patrick's Day will play out more peacefully after the UN intervened this morning. Several buses of mammies from Tyrone have just arrived in the area, and are understood to have already begun deploying anti-anti-social behaviour measures.

At the time of writing several students have had the legs beat off them with a wooden spoon, whilst riot police are also understood to have sanctioned the use of quare clip round the ear, a good skelping and a wile fierce telling-off.

Should this not be sufficient however, police do have a contingency.

'We've got a bus-load of Tyrone daddies in reserve,' explained Sergeant Tim Brass. 'They've all got their leather belts at the ready … and good boots in the hole have been authorised.'

> Several students have had the legs beat off them with a wooden spoon.

Fury at Take That star's Belfast property plans

There was anger in North Belfast this morning after it was revealed that former Take That singer Jason Orange is planning to invest over £15 million of his fortune in a new housing development in the Ardoyne area.

Mr Orange, who has moved into the property business since leaving the chart-topping group, was dismayed that his proposed development met with such an angry reaction when he unveiled his plans at a public consultation.

'I was hoping to build a small estate with the streets named after the different members of the band,' he told The Ulster Fry. 'I had Williams Avenue and Barlow Crescent, Owen Park and Donald Road on the application, and all of these were fine.'

'However when I mentioned that I also intended to have an Orange Parade in the new development the audience at the consultation went clean mental. I had to be escorted off the stage by my security staff.'

Speaking through an interpreter, Ardoyne Residents Collective spokesman Cathal O'Fended told us that the former singer's plan for the area was totally unacceptable. 'Williams Avenue is bad enough,' he said. 'That would have to be renamed Liam's Avenue, but there's no way we'll accept an Orange Parade.'

In a similarly tenuous dreamt-up story there were protests in a Ballymena branch of Tesco after Sunblest announced plans for a new range of breads named after deceased soul singers. It is understood that the shoppers were fine with the Redding Veda and Cooke soda breads, but set fire to the bakery section when someone spotted a Gay Pride loaf.

Driverless Audi to be right up your hole

Following the announcement that the UK will have a network of driverless cars by 2020, leading car manufacturers are working on software upgrades to ensure the driving experience will be as close to the real thing as possible.

'After months of trials we've finally got our A4s driving right up your hole,' confirmed Diethart Lynes from Audi. 'It will stay up your arse at top speeds and automatically flashes its lights in the fast lane to tell people to move the feck over.'

Other manufacturers are also replicating features their customers love. Driverless BMWs will not bother indicating, while the Mercedes models will automatically take up two spaces in supermarket car parks. Additionally, Fiat Unos and Nissan Micras will drive at 10 mph below the speed limit and always stop at roundabouts – even if no one is coming.

Several other car producers are also working hard. Honda, Subaru and Volkswagen are calculating a perilous overtaking algorithm, which will ensure their sporty models will fly past you at 100 mph at the most dangerous point of a country road, thus causing your arsehole to shrink to the size of a neutron in anticipation of imminent death.

Whilst driverless cars are being hailed as a revolutionary transportation breakthrough, local joyriders fear huge job losses throughout their sector.

'It's f**king bad craic,' said 19-year-old Weetabix McCafferty. 'We stole one of the prototypes from the NI Science Park, but it just drove us about at 30 mph and kept going the correct way around roundabouts. Was like being out on a driving lesson with me granda. Loada pish.'

Translink have also been experimenting with driverless buses, according to reports. In tests they kept driving past stops and ignoring passengers. 'They're perfect,' said a company spokesman.

Binmen 'plotting against you', admit council bosses

There was shock and dismay amongst ratepayers today after City Council bigwigs admitted that their refuse collectors are 'up to all kinds of stuff – none of it good'.

The news came to light after an investigation by the BBC's *Spotshite* programme revealed that binmen are secretly employed by the Department of Health to monitor the drinking habits of the average citizen. 'Most people just load up their recycling boxes and bins, and think nothing of it,' explained Belfast binman Walter Carbuncle, 'but the reality is that we keep careful records of their contents.'

Mr Carbuncle went on to reveal that, on returning to their depot, he and his fellow waste operatives fill in lengthy spreadsheets detailing the exact alcohol consumption of every household. 'We know, for example, that themuns in number forty-three go through six bottles of wine a week – usually shiraz – as well as a box of Carlsberg. Yer man tries to hide it by wrapping porn magazines around the bottles so they don't chink, and crushing the cans, but they won't get past us.'

The resulting data is then sold on to the Department of Health, where the minister is drawing up a hit list of people they suspect of being alcoholics.

This startling news was not the last revelation to emerge from the council refuse depots. Mr Carbuncle also told reporters that he and his colleagues regularly park their lorry until just before you leave for work, then drive slowly out in front of you, block the road, and proceed to spend what feels like hours manhandling bins around.

'That's not all,' he confessed. 'In stormy weather we also make sure to hide the bricks that people use to keep the lids on recycling boxes to stop them blowing down the street. That way we ensure that when folk come home the boxes have been transported several miles away, and that they then have to spend weeks getting new ones.'

We approached Belfast City Council's waste management department for comment but were told to f**k off.

Lidl leaflet voted Northern Ireland's top men's magazine

Fans of random stuff are celebrating today after the newspaper insert of German supermarket chain Lidl was revealed as the most popular reading material for men here.

Announcing the surprise choice, the chair of the Northern Ireland Publishers' Society heaped praise on the advertising sheet. 'It's something all men look forward to,' he claimed, 'settling down on the sofa with a beer to peruse the latest deals, particularly the impressive tool section.'

'I do love an impressive tool,' admitted regular reader Frank Crownfield, 'but to be honest I most look forward to the regular specials. Every now and then you get an entire section devoted to something like horses or skiing. That's what I love about Lidl, the way they have their fingers on the pulse of what their customers need – namely unusually packaged biscuits, cheap toilet roll, horse blankets and elaborate skiwear.'

Fellow reader Arnold Silvercrest is a big fan of the clothing section. 'It's the natural poses of the models that I love, as they show off the latest in budget fashions,' he explained. 'Then you might also get a wee shot of a woman in some thermal underwear, doing the ironing or something. It's titillating stuff, near as good as the bra section of the old Littlewoods' catalogues.'

However it's not just the images that appeal, as Frank explains. 'The written pieces on the items are pure poetry,' he told us. 'Just listen to this description of a bucket. *Comes with pouring spout, measuring scale and handle*. I was down there straight away; it was the mention of a handle that sold it.'

Executives from the supermarket will be presented with their gong at the star studded Ulster Men's Magazine Awards in a Ballywalter caravan park tomorrow evening. We understand that the Screwfix Catalogue scoops second place, with a slightly crumpled edition of Autotrader in third.

'I do love an impressive tool,' admitted regular reader Frank Crownfield.

Calls to end *Game of Thrones* filming after dragons torch village

There have been demands for the Stormont administration to ban the production of *Game of Thrones* here after the show's dragons accidentally set fire to much of a County Down village.

The Ulster Fry understands that the dragons escaped from their enclosure on the film set and caused massive disruption in the local area before setting fire to Corbet, a hamlet outside Banbridge.

The incident occurred at 3 a.m. this morning, when most residents were in bed. 'I was sound asleep,' says local farmer Josiah Slurry, 'when I heard all this loud screeching and the animals going buck mental in the barn. I pulled on my trousers and rushed outside. It was chaos out there – even one of the cows shat itself.'

Mr Slurry's farm was severely damaged in the blaze, and he was in no doubt about who was to blame. 'It was them dragons,' he told us. 'They're always wrecking round here – the film boys just can't seem to keep them in.'

The show's producers have admitted that they've been having 'a few issues with the cast'. Chuck Wankstein explained, 'We work long days, and at the

end of a hard filming session, everyone just wants to blow off steam. For the dragons that involves blowing fire as well.'

A spokesdragon from the animal enclosure told us that he and his colleagues were 'deeply sorry' about the incident. 'We'd been on the lash and, as usual, Geoff had one too many and yakked his hoop on the way home. Unfortunately for dragons, any boking is accompanied by a massive blast of fiery breath, and the rest is history.'

We contacted the PSNI in Banbridge and asked them if they would like to comment, but they told us to 'piss away aff' or they'd do us for wasting police time.

> ❛ We work long days, and at the end of a hard filming session, everyone just wants to blow off steam. For the dragons that involves blowing fire as well, ❜ explained producer Chuck Wankstein.

Craigavon to become 'a bit like Dubai, but with more roundabouts'

There were wild scenes of jubilation in Craigavon today as residents took to the streets to celebrate the town being crowned the 'best place to live and work' in Northern Ireland, in a survey conducted by the Post Office.

'This survey really has put Craigavon on the map ...' said councillor Wilbert Rushmere, '... somewhere between Lurgan and Portadown. Of course we locals always knew it was a hidden gem of Northern Ireland, what with its beautiful architecture, exciting nightlife and extensive collection of burned-out vehicles, but perhaps now it will get the recognition it deserves.'

The revelation has led the DETI minister to announce a multi-billion pound financial package to boost the tourism potential of the town. 'This new funding will support the erection of new luxury accommodation for visitors and residents alike,' said the minister. 'Soon we will see the world's top celebrities flock to Craigavon to experience what it means to live and work in Northern Ireland's most desirable town. It'll be a bit like Dubai, but with more flags.'

Members of the world's millionaire jet set welcomed the announcement, and promised that they would add Craigavon to their wish lists of global destinations.

Actor George Clooney told us that he'd 'never heard of Craigavon' until he read the results of the survey on the website of the *Portadown Times*. 'Me and Amal will definitely be visiting when we're over in Ireland this summer,' he said. 'We're both big fans of roundabouts, so it's a great opportunity to add to our collection.'

We also caught up with footballers Cristiano Ronaldo and Lionel Messi as they arrived at Aldergrove's Calum Best International Airport. 'We flew over this morning after last night's big match,' said Ronaldo, 'as we had read the news on Twitter. Now we are going to see if we can find a bus to take us to see this glorious city of Craigavon.'

'I am particularly looking forward to trying of this local wine you call Buckfast,' revealed his diminutive counterpart from Barcelona. 'Who knows – if we like it we may settle here and play for one of your city teams. I have always wanted to experience the atmosphere of a big derby match between Portadown and Glenavon.'

In a written statement issued through our letterbox, the Post Office has denied that they are taking the piss.

TUV start online petition to rename new Applegreen services Appleorange

Northern Ireland moved into an exciting new era this week with the opening of a petrol station at the side of a motorway. Applegreen, the roadside services chain with outlets throughout the Republic of Ireland, opened their first North of the border station on Monday, which cleverly allows cars to drive off the motorway, in one end – then out the other.

The revelation has delighted drivers leaving Belfast this week, many of whom have reported their 'amazement' at the ability to refuel a car without taking a twenty-minute detour through streets lined with spides, Icelands, sectarian murals and grotty bookmakers. 'It's class!' said local driver Donald Burmah, 'and they even take sterling! I actually took Euros just in case,' he laughed.

However, the new enterprise has not impressed TUV leader Jimbo Allister, who claims that the name 'Applegreen' is 'yet another concession to Nationalism. Seriously! Enough is enough!' declared Allister when we called to his home this morning.

After going up stairs to change out of his pyjamas the TUV chief continued, 'This new "Shared Society" is supposed to work for both communities, and yet these Republican oil barons now expect ordinary decent Unionists to spend their hard-earned cash financing the invasion of more Irish Green into our wee country! It's only common sense and fair that the name "Appleorange" would be acceptable to both communities.'

The TUV leader is now urging everyone to sign his online petition – 'Rename Applegreen Appleorange' – which he hopes will get over 100,000 signatures, so he can take the proposal to the Stormont Executive. 'Perhaps your Ulster Fry readers will get involved too!' he added.

Not to be outdone, East Belfast Sinn Féin candidate Niall Ó Donnghaile later announced a proposal to rename Orangefield Greenfield, where the party hope to 'drum up' support amongst working-class unionist voters by offering cheap laundered fuel.

Rumours about a new strain of 'Orange Diesel' remain unconfirmed at the time of going to press.

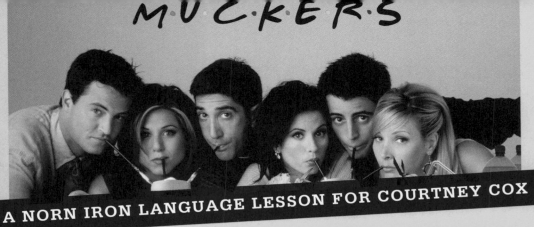

M·U·C·K·E·R·S

Yesterday we learnt that former *Friends* star Courtney Cox sometimes struggles with the accent of her Northern Irish boyfriend Johnny McDaid from Snow Patrol. We thought we'd help her out, so here's a few words she might think she knows, but that have a totally different meaning over here.

Beg
Definition: to ask someone for something formally, humbly or earnestly.
NI meaning: something in which to carry your shopping.
Usage: 'Do you wanna wee beg wi' that?'

Wan
Definition: unnaturally pale, especially from sickness or sadness etc.; the surname of a TV fashion guru.
NI meaning: the number one; a single item.
Usage: 'Gimme wan of them wee begs for my shappin.'

Lock
Definition: a device fitted to a door, drawer, lid etc. to keep it firmly closed.
NI meaning: several, a lot.
Usage: 'Gimme a lock of them begs, would ye?'

Hat
Definition: any of various head coverings, especially one with a brim and a shaped crown.
NI meaning: having a high temperature.
Usage: 'Mind you don't scald yourself on that hat watter.'

Tall
Definition: of more than average height.
NI meaning: something to dry yourself with.
Usage: 'Am going fur a shar. Have ye any talls?'

Putt
Definition: a stroke on the green with a putter to roll the ball into or near the hole.
NI meaning: to place in a particular spot.
Usage: 'Putt that shappin in the beg.'

Windy
Definition: of or relating to wind; an informal word for flatulent.
NI meaning: an opening in a wall, fitted with glass in a frame, to let light and air in, and to allow people to look out.
Usage: 'It's gettin wile windy – go and shut that windy, wud ye?'

Bake
Definition: to cook something with dry heat but no flame, typically in an oven.
NI meaning: 'beak' – face or mouth.
Usage: 'Shut yer bake before I put ye through thon windy.'

Mare
Definition: adult female horse.
NI meaning: a reflective surface, usually mounted in a frame.
Usage: 'The bake on thon doll would break a mare.'

Black
Definition: the very darkest colour.
NI meaning: to obstruct passage down something, usually a road.
Usage: 'Themuns are blacking our parade, so they are.'

This should help Ms Cox's communication skills – and if the cast of *Friends* ever gets back together for a one-off special, she can go full Norn Iron on them: 'Shut yer bake, Chandler, or ah'll stick a beg over yer head an' putt ye through thon windy, so ah will, ye ballbeg.'

Welcome to

St Bigots
School For Themuns

NI school kids 'can no longer recognise the other sort', claim teachers

There is growing concern that school children in Northern Ireland are increasingly unable to tell whether someone is Protestant or Catholic, 'just by lukkin' at them'.

A study conducted by the University of Ballywalter found that traditional skills such as 'Eye spacing' and 'Way he walks' recognition have declined markedly since the Good Friday Agreement, mainly because of a lack of contact between children from the two communities.

'In the good old days we could all tell each other apart because we'd always be sent on trips together,' says the report's author Eoin Paisley. 'But chronic lack of funding for cross-community outings has meant kids rarely get the chance to exercise these invaluable skills.

'This is compounded by the rise in naming children in a vaguely ecumenical manner,' he went on. 'There's been a huge drop in Billys, Seans, Elizabeths and Niamhs, and a surge in Jacks, Darcys, Reubens and Rhiannas. This leads to all manner of confusion when applying traditional religious recognition techniques.'

In an effort to stem the decline, the Department of Education has announced new guidelines for primary schools that insist school year books must have adequate white space under each child's photo to write 'Prod' or 'Taig' with a Crayola crayon. Meanwhile younger children will be encouraged to 'colour in' the areas in either green or orange.

'This is just one of our many initiatives to ensure our unique un-integrated education system stays ahead of the curve of moderate thinking, and instils good old fashioned notions of segregation and division into our youngsters,' said spokesman Gus Orthem today.

'Indeed we want to test our children's aptitude for telling usuns from themuns right up until they leave school,' he continued, 'with final exams and a recognised qualification to show for it.

'We're going to call them H Levels,' he revealed, 'or, if you're one of themuns, H Levels.'

> Traditional skills such as eye spacing and way he walks recognition have declined markedly since the Good Friday agreement.

NORN IRON MAN

Captured by spides in Cavehill and forced at knifepoint to chip their Sky box, Belfast electrician Tony Spark escapes by building a super-suit using his Norn Iron jersey and old parts from a 1983 Ford Cortina. He's now a champion of local football and has just bought the naming rights to Windsor Spark.

THE SILVER SLABBER

Surfing the airwaves of Ulster each morning, the Silver Slabber uses the biggest surfboard in the country to find misery in everyday situations.

THE LASH

Local student Garry Allen is transformed into super-fast Buckie drinker 'The Lash' after a freak electrical storm whilst necking a half bottle of his favourite wine.

CAPTAIN ULSTER AMERICAN FOLK PARK

Discovered foundered in the bottom of a chest freezer on the outskirts of Omagh last year, Captain Rodge Steevers now takes tourists around this famous attraction before booting them in the hole.

HAWK EYE SUR

As seen in last year's hit movie, *Avengers: Age of Ulster*, Agent Skint Barton aka 'Hawk Eye Sur' lives on a farm up the country and rounds up cattle with his trusty Bow n Arra.

DONEMANA STEEL

After crash landing in Tyrone and being adopted by the Cant family, last son of crap town, Clark Cant, turns down a job as a reporter at the Belfast Telegraph to stay on the family farm rearing cattle and holding up traffic for miles in a beat-out Massey Ferguson.

Goths outside City Hall 'planning to seize control of the council', say MI5

Sources close to the security services fear that the apparently placid gaggle of goths that hang around Belfast City Hall are, in fact, a ruthless terrorist group intent on seizing control of the city's government.

'Many of us pass them on a daily basis, and think nothing of it,' said the high-level source that we bumped into in the pub. 'But we've managed to infiltrate the group, and have discovered that for the last few months they've been secretly tunnelling under the grounds of the hall, and will soon emerge within the council chamber itself.'

'It's why they need to drink so much of that Monster energy drink, so they can do the work,' our source explained, 'and why they wear such heavy boots. Their leader is mad for health and safety so insists on protective footwear.'

Once inside a council meeting, the group plans to blow the lights and take the mayor hostage. 'They're virtually invisible in darkness, what with all the black stuff they wear,' we were told, 'and at the same time have amazing night vision developed through sitting in darkened rooms listening to Marilyn Manson. The council security folk won't stand a chance against them.'

The agent also revealed that there are several other 'high-level threats' operating in the city centre. 'That wee man outside Castlecourt with the violin-trumpet yoke? It's actually a listening device and he's working for the Russians. Then there's the boy doing the limbo dance in Cornmarket. He's a spy for the Peruvians. People don't realise what a dangerous city we live in.'

We tried to contact MI5 to confirm the story but we couldn't find them in the phone book.

Dozens arrested for using illegal electricity 'meter magnets'

Twenty-seven people were arrested across the Province this morning as part of a new PSNI operation to stamp-out the illegal 'rigging' of domestic electricity meters. The illicit practice has become increasingly popular in recent years, as NIE customers use special high-powered magnets to avail of highly illegal yet reasonably priced electricity.

Aside from the huge profit losses for Northern Ireland Electricity, the cumulative effect of so many powerful new magnets being introduced into Northern Ireland's environment has had serious repercussions right across the country.

In June last year a group of American hikers trying to reach the top of Slieve Donard ended up swimming in Lough Neagh after false compass readings threw them immeasurably off course.

Soon after, a load of classic VHS tapes safely stored in the back of a van and bound for a car-boot sale in Derry were completely erased after driving through Creggan.

The police operation that led to the arrests was made possible thanks to a new team of PSNI sniffer dogs that have been painstakingly retrained to detect the magnetic signature of tampered electricity meters.

'The process is quite time consuming,' said Jim Lorentz of the PSNI Domestic Crime Division following the arrests. 'Dogs don't really like dessert spoons being rubbed on their noses for hours on end, but the animals are not harmed in any way and the rewards speak for themselves!' Mr Lorentz went on to say that those arrested were 'in seriously hot water' – the cost of boiling which would be paid at the full Power NI tariff.

Electricity scamming is the fastest growing domestic crime in Northern Ireland, joining green/red diesel, chipped Sky boxes and counterfeit washing powder on the list of the main scourges affecting the local economy. Those arrested can now expect 'harsh financial penalties' rumoured to be somewhere in the region of actually paying for electricity.

The PSNI released a statement after the arrests: 'Ulster residents tempted to abuse their power should stop and have a word with themselves.' No Stormont ministers were available for comment as they were too busy disregarding the PSNI's advice.

Facebook.com/PureDerry

Derry
Ballymena
Belfast
Lurgan

BBC
TOPLESS SPIDE FORECAST
ULSTER BRACES ITSELF FOR SUNSHINE

14:00
WEDNESDAY

'You'll still need a coat' advises UN, as NI people strip for sunshine

The UN has stepped in to quell the overexcited behaviour that has seen people across Northern Ireland shed multiple layers of clothing at the first glimpse of the sun.

'There was a right frost his morning,' warned UN Secretary-General Ban Ki-moon, at a press conference at the Titanic Centre. 'Just because there's a drop of sun doesn't mean it'll still be warm when you head home later.'

'It's still only April, and the chances are you live somewhere like Lisburn or Derry – not Lisbon or Dubai,' he concluded. 'In short, or in shorts, catch yourselves on.'

Mothers across the country have welcomed the intervention, after many spent a harrowing afternoon watching their kids come home from school with jumpers round their heads and trousers rolled up to the knees. However it seems that many local people are refusing to heed the advice.

Twenty-three-year-old Tullycarnet man Chuck Naked told us that he'd been 'dressing for the weather' since he woke at 6 a.m. 'It was minus two when I got the bus but I thought f**k it, the sun's out, so it's taps aff tae f**k.'

'It's an ideal chance to show off my new ink,' he continued, showing us an impressive tattoo depicting

the Queen scoring for Rangers in a penalty shoot-out against Celtic.

In the northwest, Strabane man Sean O'Naturel had a similar attitude. 'I was caught out by this turn in the weather, and all I could find to wear to work was a pair of Tyrone GAA shorts from 1985. You know the wans, showed more balls than the match highlights.'

Sadly Mr O'Naturel works in Bank of Ireland and was sent home after a colleague reached for a money bag and got more than she bargained for.

According to experts the outlook for the rest of the week remains good. 'Sunny 'til the weekend,' revealed UTV weather terrorist Frank Mitchell, before baring his arse as part of an elaborate clue to a local place name.

'Can you guess where the weather watching camera is tonight?'

> ❝ It's still only April, and the chances are you live somewhere like Lisburn or Derry – not Lisbon or Dubai. In short, or in shorts, catch yourselves on, ❞ warned Ban Ki-moon.

Ulster Fry Party to field candidates in Assembly election

From the BBC News website. To be published 6 p.m.

The writers of local satirical website The Ulster Fry have revealed that they are to stand in the forthcoming Stormont election.

At a press launch in Belfast this morning the men behind the new Ulster Fry Party told reporters that they wanted to offer a genuine alternative to voters. 'We want to avoid the clichés of the past,' they explained. 'We'll be offering a shared future, in an Ireland of equals, secure within the Union, open on Sundays.

'No more Orange and Green politics – we'll be somewhere in between, which is light brown as we've checked by mixing paint.'

Key policies were also unveiled at the press launch.

• Education: support for integrated education and staggered school start/finish times to allow teenagers to spend more time in bed.

• Transport: to reduce congestion and help job seekers there will be free bus passes for all under 20s and the unemployed. Paid for by a tax on BMWs and other non-indicating vehicles.

• Health: anyone turning up at hospitals or doctors' surgeries with 'feck all wrong with them' will be fined.

• Crime: the introduction of the 'good boot up the hole' as a deterrent to anti-social behaviour.

• Culture: no more grants for sectarian murals and huge bonfires. Instead there will be money for communities where there are no murals and bonfires are limited to large barbecues.

• Parading: investment in a world-class parading stadium in the Titanic Quarter. The Paradium project will allow contentious parades and the associated protests and violence to be held off the streets – minimising disruption.

• Gay marriage: will be legalised but not compulsory.

• The economy: the abolition of VAT on crisps, beer and wine will boost 'proper pubs'. To be paid for through a tax on fancy cocktails and restaurants that don't use plates.

• Europe: the party is broadly in favour of remaining in Europe, but is open to offers from other continents.

The authors of the occasionally funny site, Billy McWilliams and Seamus O'Shea, will be standing in the Belfast East and Foyle constituencies respectively, but more candidates are expected.

'It's just ourselves for now but we're lining up a few others,' says O'Shea. 'At this point we're seeking a big name from local TV – someone like Pamela Ballantine, Jackie Fullerton or Mike Nesbitt.'

No more Orange and Green politics – we'll be somewhere in between, which is light brown as we've checked by mixing paint.

The Assembly elections are almost upon us, but there is still time for candidates to make their mark.

Working around the clock, our crack team of political analysts and researchers have uncovered the secrets to an election winning strategy in Northern Ireland.

It's much more simple than you'd think.

STICK POSTERS OF YOUR FACE ON EVERY LAMP POST YOU CAN FIND

Posters here are pretty simple – just a picture of yourself with a flag in the background. Be sure to smile inanely, even though you'll spend the next five years with a big gurn on your bake.

MAKE A RAKE OF EMPTY PROMISES ABOUT STUFF

'We will provide half a million new jobs and build a motorway to Fermanagh'. Never explain how you'll pay for things, that's for someone else to worry about. If anyone asks you about it just say something like 'that's open for discussion and we'll clarify that after the election'.

SLAG OFF YOUR NEAREST RIVAL'S EMPTY PROMISES FOR BEING UNREALISTIC

'How can they promise to create half a million new jobs and build a motorway to Fermanagh? Where are their costings?' Only your empty promises are realistic, make that clear at every opportunity.

SCARE THE VOTERS

'IF YOU DON'T VOTE FOR OUR PARTY THEN SATAN WILL RULE THE EARTH,' or similar works well. Shout 'You're not allowing me to answer the question' when anybody challenges you about it.

SLAG OFF ANY OTHER PARTIES THAT CLAIM TO REPRESENT YOUR COMMUNITY

Let's face it, if you're standing for a 'Green' or 'Orange' party, you aren't really interested in trying to persuade people from the other community that your ideas are good ones. Just have a go at the other Green or Orange parties for selling out or making unrealistic promises.

KNOCK ON PEOPLE'S DOORS AS THEY ARE JUST ABOUT TO EAT THEIR DINNER

The electorate love to see political party representatives arriving at their homes just as they're about to eat or put the kids to bed. Ask them if they have any concerns or questions then ignore what they say.

GET A GREAT RESPONSE ON THE DOORSTEPS

Everyone gets a great response even when they're told to f**k off by pensioners and bitten by children.

FINALLY, WHEN YOU DO WIN, BE REALLY GRACIOUS IN VICTORY

The Ulster Fry

Chas&Cam
Sandringham,
England

Level **3** Contributor

21 reviews

7 hotel reviews

12 helpful votes

🦉🦉 **shitadvisor**®

"Very heavy breakfast, drums too loud"

◉○○○○ *Reviewed last night*

Primarily over as a business trip, but our hosts promised to show us some of the sights. Thought we might have got to see that causeway thing, the swingy bridge and those pubs with beardy men and penny whistles you see in the adverts. Instead we saw a carpet factory, some men with sashes and the Garvaghy Road. The politicians all seemed very angry, the crisps were terribly strong and we got the impression that our hosts Arlene and Martin had been rowing all week. Still, as Camilla said, 'At least they didn't make us go to Lurgan'

Helpful?   👍Thank Chas&Cam   🚩 Report

Fury as Charles and Camilla give Northern Ireland a bad review

There was anger and dismay in tourism circles this morning after it emerged that Prince Charles had given Northern Ireland a one-star review on the popular travel site Shitadvisor.

Mr Wales has been here for a couple of days now, with his wife Camilla arriving yesterday, and it had been thought that the pair had been enjoying their mini-break. However it turns out that neither of them had been impressed with an itinerary that included several factories, an Orange Order museum and a walkabout in Portadown.

The review has had the unusual result of uniting the Province's feuding politicians. First Minister Arlene Foster was furious, complaining about 'that posh ballbag coming over here and sleggin like he thinks he owns the place'.

Meanwhile stalwart republican Martin McGuinness has also leapt to Northern Ireland's defence. 'How dare he have a go at Our Wee Country?' he tweeted. '#OrangeOrderMuseum is pure class. I've been nine times and I'm still not bored of looking at sashes.'

The offending review was swiftly deleted, but not before royal aides were forced into a gushing apology. 'Charles loves the place, honest,' said Chief Footman Windsor Castle. 'He'd had a few jars last night and was rubbered. He's always posting shite when he's pished, but usually under the alias Katie Hopkins. Though, to be fair – Portadown? What were yis thinking sending them there?'

The royal couple head on to Donegal today, leading the Prince to tweet, 'Nice landscape, shame about the Mexicans,' early this morning.

❝ He'd had a few jars last night and was rubbered. He's always posting shite when he's pished, but usually under the alias Katie Hopkins. Though, to be fair – Portadown? What were yis thinking sending them there? ❞ said Chief Footman Windsor Castle.

DUP appoints Hannibal Lecter as new Executive minister

DUP leader Arlene Foster announced a major reshuffle of her ministerial team today, in what she described as a bid to 'find the right people with the right skills for the job'.

In a headline-grabbing move, Mrs Foster has appointed Dr Hannibal Lecter as the new minister for health, highlighting the fictional cannibal's impressive medical credentials as her main motivation for the appointment. 'Dr Lecter has spent a huge amount of time in different health institutions, both in a professional and an advisory capacity. I don't know why we didn't think of him before.'

Dr Lecter has had a relatively low profile as an East Antrim MLA, but is known as a moderate within the party. His appointment follows a number of scandals involving previous health ministers, with both Jim Wells and Edwin

Poots finding themselves embroiled in allegations of homophobia. According to our DUP insider, in Dr Lecter the party believe they have a 'safe pair of hands who'll avoid any controversy'.

Speaking outside his Larne home, the new minister told reporters that he was keen to get to grips with the problems facing the health service. 'I'm really looking forward to getting my teeth into the job,' he told reporters. 'I'm making waiting lists my number one priority and I already have some mouth-watering new ideas for how to dramatically reduce hospital queues across Northern Ireland.'

As part of the post-election reshuffle the first minister has also appointed suitably qualified fictional characters to two other departments. From tomorrow, Captain James T. Kirk will take the helm at the Department of Enterprise, whilst the Count from Sesame Street will become Minister for Finance and Personnel.

Both are said to be 'relishing the opportunity', with the Count declaring that there would 'one, two, three thousand civil servants' made redundant within the next few months, before laughing maniacally as thunder clapped in the background.

Daniel Craig quits Bond to become Stormont Justice Minister

Heart-throb actor Daniel Craig has stunned movie fans by turning down a reported £68 million deal to return as James Bond, so that he can take on the role of Justice Minister for the Stormont Executive.

In an exclusive interview with The Ulster Fry, Mr Craig said he had been following developments here with interest, and he's ready to step in if the Alliance party won't take on the role.

'There'd be a few changes obviously,' he told us. 'A lot less standing about talking, and a lot more running around fighting folk whilst only wearing pants. Suffice to say I'll be dishing more boots up the hole than you got from David Ford.'

The move would certainly shake up the administration of justice here, but Sinn Féin have been quick to condemn what they regard as 'the interference of British securocrats'.

'Craig has clearly been operating a shoot-to-kill policy in his previous job,' said North Belfast MLA Gerry Kelly, who has never seen a gun in his life. 'We can't have professional killers holding positions of power here, only amateur ones.'

The news leaves Alliance in a quandary. 'They can either take the position themselves, or nominate one of their MLAs to be the next James Bond,' says political pundit Alexis Cane. 'I can't see Naomi Long in the role so that leaves Ford or Farry, though it's hard

to imagine either of those two emerging out of Belfast Lough in their budgie smugglers.'

Meanwhile Mr Craig has made a final pitch for the position, telling us, 'It's either me or that wee fecker Steven Agnew. He'd have youse all riding bikes to work, but I prefer doing my riding in work,' he concluded, before shouting yeoooooo and leaping out of the window.

The New Stormont Executive

Stormont has an Executive, finally, with brand new ministers and departments. With all the changes up on the hill it's hard for the ordinary citizen to understand what's going on, so here's our guide to who they all are, and what they'll be doing.

Executive Office:
First and Deputy First Ministers: Arlene and Marty, of course.
Responsibilities: Pretend to like each other at public events then slag each other off afterwards. Look cross.

Junior Ministers: Alastair Ross DUP and Meagan Fearon SF.
Responsibilities: Kinda like support staff for the rest. Stand beside the other ministers looking serious during the various crises that come over the next five years and make the tea at meetings.

New Executive unveiled at Stormon

Department of Education
New Minister: Peter Weir DUP.
Responsibilities: The key role of the Education Minister is to improve the educational attainment of children from whichever side of the sectarian divide they represent. Expect the return of the 11+ and lots of excuses.

Department for the Economy
New Minister: Simon Hamilton DUP.
Responsibilities: Meant to promote things like jobs and tourism, but in reality he'll spend his time at golf tournaments and smiling when crap jobs in call centres are announced, then looking sad when engineering firms close down.

Department of Finance
New Minister: Mairtin O'Millionaire SF.
Responsibilities: Supposedly controls the cash dished out to the other departments, so very important. In other words he'll share out the pocket money that Westminster gives us.

Department of Health:
New Minister: Michelle O'Neill SF.
Responsibilities: One of the most important departments, so no one wants it. Basically in charge of waiting lists.

Department of Justice
New Minister: Claire Sugden Ind.
Responsibilities: A job so divisive that neither of the big two parties trusts the other to do it, Claire's job is to be blamed for everything that involves the police.

Department for Infrastructure
New Minister: Chris Hazzard SF.
Responsibilities: Fixing potholes and cutting the grass. Will announce lots of big schemes that won't happen.

Department for Communities
New Minister: Paul Givan DUP.
Responsibilities: In most societies you'd have a Department for THE Community, but we can't have that as it might involve getting on with each other. In charge of both the Bru and Arts, oddly, Paul 'Conscience Clause' Givan is just the man for the Culture and Arts side of things.

Department of Agriculture, Environment and Rural Affairs
New Minister: Michelle McIlveen DUP.
Responsibilities: Her role will be to give out grants to keep culchie voters happy. Amusingly this department's acronym – DAERA – reads a bit like diarrhoea, if you're a big wain.

Other Duties
All ministers must remember their main responsibility – arguing on *Nolan*.

Armagh man offers to 'knock Trump's pan in'

A County Armagh man has travelled to the USA to make a unique offer to the people of that troubled country – to personally knock the smug look off Donald Trump's fat face.

Forty-eight-year-old Declan Flannery arrived in Washington early yesterday morning, and is understood to be 'looking for a lift to wherever Trump is' so he can administer a severe beating.

Before he left for the States, Mr Flannery told The Ulster Fry that he'd been troubled for some time by an age old philosophical question. 'If you could travel in time, would you go back to 1933 and kick in Hitler's ring piece?' he asked us. 'In my opinion, if the Nazi leader had been given

a severe boot up the hole before he seized power we might have avoided World War Two.

'It's difficult for the American people to deal with Trump so I'll knock his pan in for them,' he continued. 'Then I'll stick every brick of that wall he's always on about up his cavernous arse, and make him pay for it.'

This is not the first time that the former farm labourer has offered to physically assault an international political figure. In 1989 he was widely credited with bringing down the Berlin Wall after he 'battered the melt' out of East German dictator Erich Honecker.

For now, however, Mr Flannery must wait on the decision of the American people. 'I can't go around

kicking the shite out of people without a democratic mandate,' he explained. 'I'll have to wait and see how many likes and shares my "I'll knock Trump's pan in" Facebook page gets.'

A spokesman for America told us that they'd consider the offer, but there was a long queue of people wanted to punch the presidential hopeful's gub and Mr Flannery must wait his turn.

Local man who leaves doors open was actually born in a field

A thirty-four-year-old Dungiven man has opened his soul to The Ulster Fry, revealing the living hell that the circumstances of his birth created.

Joel McCafferty is tired of being hounded for not closing doors behind him. We met up with him in a field where he told us of his battle to get his non-closure of doors recognized as a medical condition.

'I'm proud to have been born in a field,' said a defiant McCafferty. 'My ma ran out of petrol driving to the hospital, so pulled in to a field and delivered me herself. No mean feat in a dark, dung-covered meadow.'

McCafferty suffers from a lack of self-confidence after being constantly reminded of his fieldly roots. 'Most people who know me accept me for who I am but

meeting new people is difficult – it's especially embarrassing with ladies I bring home from the disco…

'They look at me like I'm a serial killer when they see I've no internal doors. It'd be the opposite if that was the case – I'd probably have more doors with locks and that.'

Being born in a field is taboo in modern Ireland as it evokes connotations of rural poverty. However, until the 1950s field births were a regular occurrence – so regular, in fact, that cows and sheep became accustomed to helping by boiling water and getting clean towels ready.

In 2004, Joel was humiliated out of his hometown after being caught 'having a sit-down visit' with the door open in the pub. It was a bank holiday and the place was packed for a Guns 'N' Roses tribute band from Newry.

'Normally I'm sure to poo before I go out but for some reason that day it wasn't coming. I should have just had a smoke and a coffee on the bog to help things but I'd a coort arranged and was late. Love does that to you.'

Once word of his disgrace got out, all hope of a local wife evaporated, and Joel moved to Magherafelt where he has now set up a support group for fellow strugglers.

'The Magherafelt Field Birth Society is very inclusive,' he told us. 'If any one shares this problem, our door is always open.'

> Until the 1950s field births were a regular occurrence – so regular, in fact, that cows and sheep became accustomed to helping by boiling water and getting clean towels ready.

Edwin Poots unveils 'sexy' new restaurant franchise for Norn Iron

DUP stalwart Edwin Poots stunned the local business community today by announcing a 'sexy' new restaurant franchise for a modern-day Northern Ireland.

Eponymously named 'Pooters', the fast food chain intends to set pulses racing amongst God-fearin' Ulster voters, thanks to a bevy of over-adequately clad waitresses, who will serve food whilst provocatively parading around in ankle-length skirts and heavy starched blouses with long sleeves, which have been tantalisingly buttoned to the neck.

'Our party has gained a bad rap the last few years,' explained Poots today at the launch. 'We've objected to a late-night lap-dancing club in Belfast, made a huge fuss over gay blood, banned same-sex marriage and refused to budge on legalised abortion … so people harshly peg us as being out-of-touch old fuddy-duddys,' he lamented.

'This new chain restaurant, though, which has the full endorsement of my party, will finally show the world that we know how to let our hair down … Well, except for the women,' he added quickly. 'They'll need to keep theirs tied up tightly, under a cloth cap.'

The closed-doors private launch of Pooters reportedly went down a storm amongst party delegates, who could barely pay attention to their food, as a slew of sexy waitresses flashed their bare wrists and ankles at every opportunity.

The Pooters menu includes a range of delicious local seafood dishes such as cod-fearing soul, the fishionary position and I'm going to eel for this, as well as some foreign dishes including prime American Trump steaks, platters of flaming hot right-wings and steak & no-McGuinness pie.

This isn't the first time a local politician has moved into fast food, of course. In 1992 Gerry Adams opened a fried chicken outlet in West Belfast. He still denies it to this day.

BABY'S FIRST BONFIRE

"SURE WHERE'S THE HARM IN IT?"

INCLUDES

2000 MINI
WOODEN PALLETS

THON FOREIGN FLEG

PLYWOOD TO BOARD
UP YOUR WINDYS

ASSORTED OFFENSIVE
SPRAY STENCILS

BOX OF MATCHES

MATCHBOX

CONTENTIOUS ROUTE

MARCHOPOLY

BREXIT SURVIVAL
MOVE TO STRABANE
GET BLOCKED
RIDE A BIKE TO WORK
EAT PASTIE SUPPERS

Summer

‘ The entire city of Belfast is to be dismantled and moved to a new location to allow the construction of a massive loyalist bonfire. ’

Drink smuggling getting harder, say wedding guests

The Irish wedding industry faces a crisis today, amid concerns that sneaking cheap drink into hotels is becoming increasingly difficult – after another weekend of boozy wedding receptions across the country.

Guests at weddings have noted alarming numbers of dirty looks from hotel staff in comparison to previous summers, with several reports of wedding celebrations being ruined by newfangled car park CCTV systems and annoying 'jobsworth' bouncers.

'After buying a dozen rounds of drinks at a wedding reception most people have had enough' – said Paddy Jameson from Lurgan – 'of paying their ridiculous hotel bar prices, I mean! It's not healthy for anyone's bank balance to fork out for whiskies until 6 a.m. There's no harm in sneaking in a couple of litres of spirits for a wee nightcap.'

Several recent wedding guests we contacted confirmed that over-zealous hotel staff had spoiled their friends' big days out this year too. 'I put a lot of time and money into preparing for my friends' weddings,' protested Glen Fiddich from Omagh. 'I only fill my car boot with the bottled beer they actually sell at the hotel bar,

and them hip flasks are expensive on eBay. Them bouncers who stopped me are dicks.'

As hotels beef up security, guests are now resorting to ridiculous methods for getting booze into weddings. 'We've started giving away carry-outs as presents,' admitted Tina Colada from Cookstown. 'Then we buy it back off them for cash. It's a handy way to give the bride and groom money whilst getting booze in at the same time … and it's far handier than baking a magnum of vodka into the wedding cake. Trust me on that.'

One long-standing local wedding tradition seems to be unaffected by the clampdown, though. 'Aye, we're still getting in bags of coke easy enough,' admitted everyone whilst blocked.

Sir Van Morrison set to smile on next album

Following years of speculation, the music industry was abuzz today with the news that, following his recent knighthood, legendary Belfast musician Sir Van Morrison is set to smile on his next album.

Morrison, famous for such classic hits as 'Moondance', 'Brown Eyed Girl' and 'Days Like This', hasn't smiled in public in almost thirty years, with the last reported sighting being at a passport photo-booth in Dundonald Ice Bowl – a claim the singer still strenuously denies.

Van is no stranger to innovation, though, having constantly reinvented himself in a fifty-year career that has seen him master rock, blues, jazz – and even country. This year is no different, it seems, with the reclusive singer

set to take on his most ambitious project yet – by forming his mouth into a shape that gives the impression he is having fun.

Morrison, who once famously won a staring contest with a painting of himself, set the rumour mill alight with his plans to grin, after he was spotted buying Colgate Extra White in the Poundland in Ann Street in preparation for his upcoming trip to Buckingham Palace.

Not seeming miserable is a radical new direction for the East Belfast songster, with other experimental upbeat collaborations rumoured to include a nod and a wink with Sir Tom Jones, a handshake with Jools Holland, a thumbs-up to KT Tunstall and a fist-bump with John Legend.

Rumours of a bonus twerk-track with Miley Cyrus so far remain unconfirmed.

His agent denied the news, though, saying that Morrison had actually laughed at the suggestion he would be seen smiling in public.

No one believed him.

Morrison once famously won a staring contest with a painting of himself.

The Sound of Stormont set for world tour

A new musical set in the heady world of Northern Irish politics is set to take the theatre industry by storm when it makes its debut in London's West End next week.

Described as a 'radical reworking of a family favourite', *The Sound of Stormont* features many of our best-loved MLAs as they endeavour to find something useful to do during their summer recess.

The show sees Peter Robinson take on the role of Baron von Crapp, a stern-faced retired admiral who is struggling to bring up a large family in his big house on the hill. The Baron decides he needs help, and takes on a young au pair called Martina (Martin McGuinness) – a former novice nun with the Armalite Sisters. Soon, the two find themselves at the centre of a titanic struggle as the English Nasty Party attempts to persuade them to introduce welfare reform.

However it's the songs that have had the critics drooling. 'I love what they've done with the old *Sound of Music* numbers,' the *Daily Telegraph*'s Hermione Silverspoon told us. '"How do you solve a problem like Jim Allister?" is beautiful, and when Arlene Foster leads the von Crapp family in the song "Sixteen Going on Ninety" it just melts the heart.'

Some other leading MLAs get their own numbers, with Gerry Kelly crooning 'Climb Ev'ry Land Rover' and Gregory Campbell belting out 'Do-Re-My Yoghurt'. Little Paul Givan's rendition of 'I Have Conscience Clause' has been singled out for praise, but the ensemble's reworking of the classic 'Edelweiss' as 'Idleshites' has been described as the highlight of the show.

The Sound of Stormont begins its world tour at London's Old Vic this Friday. Tickets start at £16.90 for the stalls, 'rising' to £19.16 for those in the balcony. There will be no concessions.

> The reworking of 'Edelweiss' as 'Idleshites' is the highlight of the show.

Height of speed bumps dictated by shiteness of housing estates, admits DOE

Minister for the Environment Mark Humpty Durkan today revealed the shocking truth of how his department decides on the height of speed bumps in housing estates around Northern Ireland.

'Many factors are used to calculate the altitude of annoying tarmac obstructions in your area,' revealed Durkan, 'but the likelihood of some spidey wee hoor kicking the wing mirrors off your car, syphoning off your home heating oil or driving a quad bike through your garden on the way to the chippy are the most decisive,' he confessed.

The science behind the grading of speed bumps has long perplexed drivers around the Province, who for years have noted the variety of driving styles needed to drive through Ulster's housing estates. Whilst some speed bumps can be driven over with relative ease, others require skilled off-road expertise to navigate and sometimes appear on Ordnance Survey maps of Northern Ireland.

'We hast come here to climb ze mountain of Slieve Donard' said a confused Heinrich Flugglehauffen as he stood atop a speed bump in the middle of the Rathcoole Estate whilst carefully inspecting an upside-down map. 'Over here, Heinrich, I think I've found it, ja,' shouted his wife in German (which we don't understand a word of, but amazingly were able to quote in this article in readable English). 'I think I've found it,' she squealed, as she dragged her backpack to the top of a huge tarmac mound forty feet away and took out a packed lunch.

In Durkan's home town of Derry this revelation seemed glaringly obvious after it was pointed out that the Royal Mail was now delivering letters to the Creggan Estate in a monster truck. 'Aye, eighties TV enthusiasts will be pleased to know that fan favourite "Bigfoot" is now in action as a post van in Derry,' said Royal Mail worker Ann Velope. 'It's already saved us a fortune in van repairs – plus we fill him up over the border with green diesel!'

The news has shed light on other peculiar vehicles that have been seen in action across the country. 'I've always wondered why the NI mountain rescue team were going door to door selling spuds, eggs and veg,' said Lurgan resident Tenzing McConkey. 'And I just assumed Dominos delivering in an army tank was part of some odd marketing ploy – but now it all makes sense.'

Most shockingly, in more affluent areas such as Bangor, Hillsborough and Holywood, the DOE have admitted that they 'just paint white squares on the road' in an effort to appear fair and equal to everyone. 'To be honest, some of these places are that rich and swanky that we've been able to invert our traffic calming measures to a dip in the road,' said Normal Maxwell from the DOE.

'We call them speed troughs,' he added.

The Royal Mail is now delivering letters to the Creggan Estate in a monster truck.

HOW TO SURVIVE THE BALMORAL SHOW

The Balmoral Show was invented in 1896 to allow folk from the sticks to look at 'yos an' coos' whilst at the same time being in 'the big smoke'.

However it has now moved to Lisburn, much to the delight of Belfast people, who no longer have to spend three days stuck in heavy traffic while farmers drive at three miles an hour waving to each other and occasionally stopping for a conversation on the Westlink. It remains a great day out for everyone, not just culchies, so we've done a handy wee guide on Balmoral etiquette for anyone thinking of popping along for the first time.

1. WHAT TO WEAR
Ideally three coats and a V-neck jumper, a flat cap and Welly boots. Not fancy coloured ones, black, with muck on them. A shirt is optional. Baler-twine belts used to be the style, but give off a country bumpkin look, so you're better off with a pair of braces. For women, much the same look,

but wear a dress under the jumper. Both sexes should carry a stout stick at all times.

2. FOOD
A true culchie won't waste his money on the 'overpriced brock' on offer – he brings his own sangwiches, in a Mother's Pride bag or an an old shortbread tin. However, if you're smart you can survive for next to nothing, mainly by consuming the free Veda, yogurts and milk

that get dished out. Buying the odd poke is essential though, even if it's pishing.

3. WHAT TO DRIVE
In an ideal world a Massey Ferguson 135 circa 1965. If not, a 1987 Landrover Defender with a

sheep in the back. Basically any yoke built before 1995 that has muck on it and its spare wheel on the outside.

4. POLITICIANS
Politicians of all shades love the Balmoral Show, except the Alliance (who are too townie), and the Greens (who would be shot). Avoid them at all costs, you might end up getting your photy tuck and accidentally find yourself in a

Sinn Féin or DUP political broadcast sometime. Here, Jim Allister photobombs some cattle.

5. WHAT TO SAY
'Grawnd day fur it.'
'Luk at the udders on thon cutty.'
'Where is the grant tent?'
'Dae ah git a free Newsletter wi' that?'
'When is Hugo Duncan oan?'
'Ah am aff fur til luk at them new Rennold tractors.'

6. WHAT NOT TO SAY
'The boys and I come here every year, it is important for them to understand where their food comes from.'
'Is there a vegetarian option?'
'Renault'

Ards woman hospitalised after being asked to pay at shop till

A 47-year-old Newtownards woman is said to be in a 'stable but critical' condition after she was asked to pay for her shopping in the town's branch of Asda.

Eye-witnesses say that the woman, named locally as Donna Caddee, stood watching as the assistant scanned her shopping at the till, but appeared completely bewildered and unprepared when she was then asked to pay.

'The girl said, "That'll be £24.50 so it will," and yer woman just stared at her like she wasn't expecting it,' said fellow shopper Rab O'Tower. 'Then she starts hoking in her handbag looking for her purse under all the make-up and shite that women always seem to carry.

'This went on for a good five minutes, but even when she managed to hand over the money she started pulling out voucher after voucher and getting the girl to check them,' Mr O'Tower continued. 'Most of them seemed to be for things she hadn't bought, or they'd expired in 1984. It was a complete pantomime.'

After eventually paying Mrs Caddee struggled to her car where she passed out from exhaustion.

The Ulster Hospital's Dr Crawford Burn-Beach says these types of incidents are not uncommon. 'We call it Anti-Social Shopper Syndrome,' he told us. 'It's basically a condition which makes you a complete arsehole when you're out shopping.'

Other symptoms include suddenly remembering something as you're about to pay and having to run to the far end of the shop, standing talking to your friend in the middle of the aisle, and taking twenty minutes to choose cheese so that no one else can reach the counter.

Away from supermarkets sufferers are also prone to parking at the petrol station's only diesel pump before going inside to do their weekly shop, and urgently needing to rearrange the contents of their wallets whilst standing at the cashpoint.

Fortunately, Dr Burn-Beach says that there is a cure. 'Aye, it's easy dealt with,' he told us. 'It's nothing a good boot up the hole wouldn't sort out.'

> Sufferers are also prone to parking at the petrol station's only diesel pump before going inside to do their weekly shop.

'What Royal Honour?' says Gerry Adams CBE

There is growing consternation in republican circles today amid rumours that several senior members of Sinn Féin, including leader Gerry Adams, have accepted awards in the Queen's Birthday Honours list.

The information came to light after Mr Adams tweeted a photo of himself alongside Deputy First Minister Martin McGuinness, in which the two men appear to have royal honours pinned to their lapels.

According to heraldry experts Mr McGuinness is wearing a British Empire medal, while the Sinn Féin leader has the Commander of the British Empire award.

The offending tweet was subsequently deleted, and Mr Adams has been quick to pour cold water on the story. In a written statement the Louth TD states, 'I am not, and never have been, a Commander of the British Empire. I've never even been a Member of the British Empire, although I did spend some time at Her Majesty's Pleasure during the 1970s. These scurrilous rumours are designed to discredit me and destabilise the peace process.'

However the denial is cutting little ice with some of his fellow republicans. Former 'blanketman' Francis 'the Fox' McLaughlin, who shared a bathtub with Mr Adams in the Maze Prison in 1974, told us, 'Gerry is always denying stuff. I lent him a tenner in the pub two months ago and now he says that although he is proud to be associated with that pub, he was never in it and never got a tenner off me. I've even heard that Gerry Kelly has been awarded the Queen's Police Medal, something to do with him fixing the wipers on a Land Rover during a riot. I don't know what to believe anymore.'

A spokesman for Buckingham Palace has stated that the Queen refuses to comment on individual awards, but he did confirm that no honour had been conferred on former First Minister Peter Robinson. 'Her Majesty did not call him a "Count",' he stated. 'She was misheard.'

> ❛ I've even heard that Gerry Kelly has been awarded the Queen's Police Medal, something to do with him fixing the wipers on a Land Rover during a riot, ❜ Francis 'the Fox' McLaughlin told us.

Euros crisis as IFA accidentally order 'non-iron shirts' for squad

With Euro 2016 just days away, the IFA have dealt Northern Ireland fans a huge blow by announcing they mistakenly requested a consignment of wrinkle-free formal shirts instead of the team's official football jersey.

'Due to a communication mix-up when ordering we've received a container of "non-iron" shirts instead,' explained IFA Chief Executive Patrick Nelson earlier. 'The guys at Adidas are extremely apologetic, but it's too late to replace the order now, so we'll have to make do.

'Seems asking Germans for "Norn Iron shirts" in a Belfast accent is a recipe for disaster,' he added.

Both the players and fans are now resigned to making the best of the situation. The IFA called in the services of grannies across NI, who stayed up all night sewing NI badges onto the shirts in time for the tournament.

'I got mine this morning,' said Hans Kerchief from Bangor. 'And whilst it isn't quite what I hoped to be wearing to cheer the lads on, the fact I didn't have to iron it was a real bonus. Plus I can wear it into work or a swanky restaurant and no one bats an eyelid.'

Michael O'Neill now faces a huge selection headache ahead of the opening game against Poland. 'I can't decide between the light-blue pin stripe with the double cuff, or the plain white slim-fit with button-down collar,' he told us.

'The lads are taking it well though,' he continued. 'They tried them on earlier and they were roaring with laughter. Ye might even say they were in creases about it, but the truth is that it didn't take a wrinkle out of them.'

The IFA now plan to use the new formal attire to their advantage. 'We're insisting the team wears a neck accompaniment with two embroidered photos of our home ground on it,' continued Nelson.

'So, a home tie?' we asked, anticipating a punchline.

'No,' he answered. 'A double Windsor.'

Prince George 'sick of dressing like it's 1953'

In an exclusive interview with The Ulster Fry, well-known toddler Prince George has revealed that he's fed up with wearing his granda's old clothes and 'wants to wear superhero stuff'.

The shock admission follows a series of photos showing the young prince poncing about in little shorts with matching jackets, cardigans and sailor suits. 'It's not my style at all,' he told us, 'I'm not even three yet FFS, and I'm ganching about dressed like some kind of weird baby throwback from a hundred years ago.'

'I'd far rather be wearing a Spider-Man outfit like my mates down at playgroup, or maybe a nice T-shirt with a dinosaur on it. I like dinosaurs, Triceratops is my favourite cos he has three horns for no apparent reason. But instead my ma is hoking through Granda Charlie's old stuff and

making me look like a right eejit.'

Prince Baby George was particularly disgruntled at appearing in his jammies with President Obama. 'All the lads in the park will see it, so I'll get quare stick on the swings. It's OK for Charlotte, she's a girl and they like dressing up as princesses, but it's different for me.'

George also told us that he was worried about his birthday in July. 'Wait 'til you see the cut of me.

She'll probably have me dressed in a top hat and tails and having tea with King Philippe of Belgium. I'd far rather be down the jungle gym having a feed of Skips with the lads. Then we could all boke over each other in the ball pit and stick Lego up our noses like normal kids.

'It's a completed shitemare being a Prince,' he concluded. 'Speaking of which, how are youse at changing nappies?'

UN aid convoy brings clean underwear to Irish fans trapped in France

The UN has stepped in to avert 'a potential humanitarian crisis' by bringing much needed supplies to fans of Northern Ireland and the Republic stranded in France.

Now two weeks in, it is understood that many fans are running low on essentials, including underwear, Veda bread, flags and Buckfast.

One stranded member of the Green and White Army told us that the crisis was of a biblical scale. 'There's thousands of us wandering the streets unable to communicate with the locals outside of "quatre bières s'il vous plait" and "Will Grigg est en feu",' explained Antrim man Gary Armstrong. 'I ran out of pants on Monday but I've met one lad from Larne who's been wearing the same pair for a week, though he says that's pretty normal for Larne.'

Lurgan man Shea Houghton told us Republic fans were experiencing similar difficulties. 'We used our last pair of clean underbags on Monday to clean the windscreens of passing French cars whilst pissed for a YouTube video. We've been going commando ever since. If French people thought there was "some craic" at the Italy match, wait 'til they see us on Sunday!'

Food is an issue too. 'We haven't eaten properly in days,' said NI Fan, Beef Gillespie. 'There's only so much pain you can take: pain au chocolat, pain aux raisins, petit pain … We need proper food – crisp sandwiches and sausage sodas.'

Such dire stories have forced the UN to take action, with a huge aid convoy currently en route from Rosslare. Planes have also been dropping pastie baps and cases of Harp by parachute. However a mix-up with flag-drop parcels could see Northern Ireland cheered on against Wales with Tricolours, whilst the Republic may face France to the backdrop of a sea of Ulster flegs.

However, rather than using the mix-up as a reason for violence, Irish fans were so sound that they had simply organised a 'Flegs for Clean Begs' exchange programme.

However, there's one further difficulty facing our brave fans. 'I know why they are called the Euros now,' explained skint fan Randy Townsend. 'Cos ye need a whole f**king rake of them. Ma, if you're reading this, send us a sub.'

Buying Primark clothes now cheaper than doing a wash

With families still finding it tough to make ends meet, a recent survey has revealed that doing a wash has become so ridiculously expensive that many mums are now forced to buy new clothes from Primark instead.

'Have you seen the price of a big box of Daz now?' complained Melinda Zannussi, a mother of 3–4 children from Lurgan. 'When the girl at the checkout told me how much I owed I literally shat myself. So I went across to Primark instead and bought six pairs of nags, some pyjamas and a bedspread. Then I went home and cried myself to sleep."

'My tears removed a stubborn make-up stain from my favourite pillow,' she added with an ironic smile.

Fellow housewife Rachael Servis agreed. 'Surf costs more than broadband now. We put what little spare money we have towards multipacks of socks, underbags and T-shirts with stupid writing on them. There is a huge mountain of laundry piling up in the spare room, like, but if God spares us, the Credit Union will give us a loan next year to do a big wash.'

'It's not just the price the washing powder,' added Judith Indesit, a 28-year-old mother of several small people covered in chocolate. 'The electric costs a fortune too. I put a load on last week and it left me with 72p on my meter. I had to watch Jeremy Kyle through the neighbours' window for the rest of the week to ration it 'til pay day. You'd think thon cheapskate would pay a f**king window cleaner – her windys are boggin.'

Local economist Ben Whirlpool confirmed that 'the Primark effect' has hit washing powder sales hard across the Province. 'Money is tight, so lots of families are clothing themselves from piles of crunchy brown bags laying around their house. And then, when they eventually get sick of re-wearing the same underwear, they head to Primark,' he added.

Gay blood set to be 'fabulous', say medical experts

After years of being oh so negative about blood, Northern Ireland's politicians deigned to exist in the twenty-first century for a short moment today when they agreed to bring the country's laws on blood donation into line with the rest of the UK.

However, while most of the population had suspected that the DUP were opposed to gay blood because they are feckless cretins, we can exclusively reveal that they knew all along that it was 'quare gear', and planned to keep it all for themselves.

'Gay blood is known to have higher concentrations of special "pink" blood cells,' says Professor Quentin Darling from Queen's University. 'These increase oxygen flow to the brain, resulting in improved interior design skills, a better taste in clothing and an innate understanding of how to cook seafood.'

Secret transfusions given to DUP members at a lab in Lisburn yielded remarkable results, according to Darling. 'Not only did subjects turn up on the second day with better shoes, but most of them accessorised really well. Arlene had hoped to use the stuff to infuse some style and sophistication into the party, on the down-low.

'I suppose it explains the DUP's deep-seated love of fancy dress musical theatre,' concluded Darling. 'Or "parading", as they like to call it.'

However it appears they were rumbled by the Shinners. 'I knew they were up to something,' said Sinn Féin's Martin McGuinness. 'Lots of attractive women I know suddenly thought it was fashionable to have a platonic DUP friend. If it wasn't Simon Hamilton giggling with Elle McPherson in the corner, it was Paul Givan having a heart-to-heart with Cindy Crawford about her troubled love life. It would fry your head!'

However one observer told he isn't surprised by the news. 'Sure they are always slabbering they have the biggest man date in the country.'

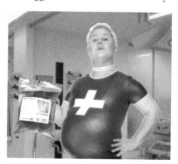

DUP knew it was 'quare gear' all along and planned to keep it for themselves.

BREXIT SURVIVAL
MOVE TO STRABANE
GET BLOCKED
RIDE A BIKE T[...]ORK
EAT PASTIE SU[...]RS

HOW TO SURVIVE BREXIT – AN ULSTER FRY GUIDE

There's turmoil in the financial markets, politicians are resigning left, right and centre, and no one seems to know whether we're in, out or kinda half way out with our mammy saying you can't go without a coat. However there are things we can all do to lessen the impact of the crisis – here's our guide to help you survive.

GET DRUNK
Everything looks better when you're in the pub, but unfortunately this is likely to be more expensive as European booze will go up in price. However we can still drink English wines and beers like Concorde and Carling – and of course there's always Buckfast.

HOLIDAY AT HOME
It's now going to cost a bomb to go abroad so it'll be cheaper to stay here and sit in a caravan looking at rain. You can still have a good time of course, visiting places like Craigavon and enjoying the traffic.

GET A BIKE
Normally The Ulster Fry wouldn't advocate this as it involves exercise, but it looks like fuel will be much dearer because of the weak pound and increased tax to help pay for farmers. You'll probably look shit in Lycra but cycling will save you a clean fortune in the Brexitpocalypse, although a bike isn't great for running over the inevitable zombies.

EAT LOCAL FOOD
Like drink, foreign food is probably going to get more expensive so save money by avoiding fancy European meals like French fries and pasta and eat chips and spaghetti hoops instead.

DON'T GET OLD
Old people voted Leave in big numbers but they'll be facing falling pensions and higher prices. It'll also be harder for retired folk to escape by going to Spain, in fact the chances are the ones living there will get sent back home to suffer from chronic Sangria withdrawal. Best to die before retirement or you'll be a burden.

MOVE TO STRABANE
Economists are predicting a drop of up to 10 per cent in average house prices in the coming months. If you live in London or North Down this equates to £50,000 so if you move to Strabane now you'll only lose £12.43.

GET AN IRISH PASSPORT
Having an Irish passport means you'll be able to act like a European when travelling, though you'll have to pretend to like their Tayto when you're going through customs. Any Unionists troubled by getting one can tippex the word 'Northern' above 'Ireland' on the front, then slip it into a British passport cover.

Police investigating multiple conflicting 'best daddy in the world' claims

After a busy morning in which almost everyone posted heart-warming Father's Day messages on social media, Interpol and the PSNI have announced that they are setting up a joint task force to get to the bottom of multiple conflicting claims of people saying their daddy is 'the best in the world'.

'Clearly someone is lying here,' said Detective Inspector Ted Sockfluff from the PSNI. 'Many citizens have made some fairly audacious claims today about the world class stature of their daddy's daddying skills – and yet others have countered by claiming exactly the same thing just minutes later. Like seriously, what is going on? We're worried it's a new threat from ISIS or something.'

The Advertising Standards Authority has also been alerted and big changes are now expected for future Father's Days.

'This is a blatant breach of advertising standards and so from next year you'll not be able to claim your daddy is "the best in the world" – unless he's got a certificate to prove it,' said Rod Anus from ASA.

'Instead you'll need to do something similar to what Carlsberg do in their advertising – and claim that your da is "probably" the best in the world. Or "allegedly brilliant" or some other shite.'

Facebook would not be drawn on the legal drama, but did reveal who they thought the best daddy in the world was based purely on site traffic.

'Father's Day posts about 52-year-old Martin Dicksplash from Craigavon got the most likes, comments and shares today,' revealed Mark Zuckerberg. 'Loads of people even left a rake of them new heart yokes we added a lock of months ago. So statistically speaking, he's the best daddy in the world.

'However I read through his private messages a few mins ago and he's a feckin head melter … so be f**ked if I know!'

Donald Trump vows to build wall around Lisburn

US Presidential hopeful Donald Trump has stirred further controversy by telling a packed audience in New York that he'd build a wall around the Northern Ireland town of Lisburn.

'We will build a wall around Lisburn, and we will make Lisburn pay for it,' he promised the crowd. 'For too long these people have been able to wander about with impunity, causing traffic jams in Belfast and banging on about how they're from a city when it's as much a city as my hole.'

Trump's campaign team appears to be gambling on the fact that absolutely no one sees the point in Lisburn, least of all the people who live there.

'Aye, it's fair enough. Even I get confused when I'm in the back arse of nowhere and get a sign saying Welcome to the City of Lisburn,' said local woman Lisa Garvey. 'I just hope they paint it a nice colour, maybe Elephant's Breath, that's what I have in my kitchen. It really matches the units. So it does.'

Her neighbour Barry McCash was also resigned to his city's fate. 'Hopefully I'll be out when they build it and I'll get to live somewhere more vibrant and interesting, like Dromore, or maybe Rathfriland,' he told us.

The announcement has proven a real shot in the arm for Mr Trump's campaign with polls showing an immediate surge in support for the disgraced candidate.

Hillary Clinton's team are reeling, with some suggesting she may be forced to stand aside if she can't reveal a similarly popular proposal at tonight's debate, such as a plan to build an electric fence around Lurgan.

Meanwhile officials at Stormont have been left bewildered by the scheme, although it's believed they'll agree so long as Hillsborough and Jeffrey Donaldson are included.

> Trump's campaign team appears to be gambling on the fact that absolutely no one sees the point in Lisburn, least of all the people who live there.

Amazonian tribe discovered living on Craigavon roundabout

There have been renewed calls for the Department for Infrastructure to improve its management of grass verges amid claims that a 'lost Amazonian tribe' is living on a roundabout in Craigavon.

The news came to light after a police helicopter patrolling the area was pelted with spears and stones as it flew over the town's picturesque Roundabout Number Six. 'We were heading to Costa at the Rushmere Shopping Centre when we came under sustained attack,' Sergeant Bobby Peeler told us. 'At first we thought it was just the locals, but when we zoomed in with the camera it turned out to be a load of boys with bones through their noses dressed in loin cloths, angrily waving spears at us outside some mud huts.

'To be honest, that didn't really provide conclusive proof that they weren't locals,' he continued, 'so after a coffee we contacted experts at Queen's University.' An expedition to explore the roundabout was organised, and early radio transmissions from the intrepid academics seemed to confirm that there is indeed a primitive Amazonian tribe resident on the roundabout. Sadly all contact was lost with the explorers several days ago, leading to fears for their safety. 'God knows what's happened to them,' says a sceptical Sergeant Peeler. 'It wouldn't be the first case of cannibalism in Craigavon.'

'The situation is critical,' Upper Bann MLA Pampas Nettle told us. 'As well as the Amazonian tribe we've had reports of wild animals living in the grass verges in the district. I'm told it's like *Jurassic Park* on the road to Gilford.'

'The whole country is going to shit,' admitted Department for Infrastructure spokesman Gordon Pothole, 'but if you read the local papers you'd think the only problem we have here is that the grass on roundabouts and verges hasn't been trimmed recently. MLAs love that kind of issue, as it allows them to complain a lot and that makes it look as if they're doing something.'

The department has now issued every MLA with a petrol strimmer and a high-vis vest. 'We might as well get a day's work out of them, and they can let on to be serving the community for a change,' said Mr Pothole.

❛ I'm told it's like *Jurassic Park* on the road to Gilford, ❜ reported Upper Bann MLA Pampas Nettle.

Belfast's Lord Mayor arrested for not paying City Hall TV licence

Sinn Féin Lord Mayor of Belfast, Harder Arson, has sensationally appeared before local magistrates this morning – charged with not paying the TV licence for the big screen outside the City Hall.

'He just told me straight to my face they didn't have a TV then slammed the door,' licensing collector John Baird told the court this morning. 'Talk about a brass neck! It's fifty-feet high and sitting out in his garden, FFS.'

Baird went on to tell the jury how, over the course of the next few days, Mr Arson concocted a string of 'lame excuses' in an effort to avoid paying. 'First he told me it had no aerial and they only used it for watching DVDs, but I wasn't buying that. The next day he told me it was just a digital photo frame for showing off his holiday snaps. Right enough, when I looked up there was a big slideshow of him in Benidorm with his missus, wearing a set of budgie smugglers. I was traumatised, but vowed to return.

'When I called back, he said the TV had been taken away, and I believed him cos it seemed to have gone. However when I got up close, I realised he'd simply uploaded a photo of the Apartment Bar so that the screen blended into the background. It was like something outta *Mission Impossible*!'

After weeks of playing cat and mouse Mr Arson was eventually caught out. 'I knocked at his door one sunny day and asked him to explain why there were hundreds of goths lying on his front lawn watching the Wimbledon tennis final on BBC 1.'

The Mayor is officially the first member of Sinn Féin to pay his TV licence – a move since heralded as a 'brave step towards peace' by Martin McGuinness. However the party was quick to reassure its electorate that by paying the licence they were in no way recognising the right of the BBC to show TV programmes on Irish soil, apart from *Eastenders*, *Homes Under the Hammer* and 'anything with Ainsley Harriott'.

> 'Why were there hundreds of goths watching the Wimbledon final on his front lawn?'

Hillsborough voted 'town most up its own hole' by tourist chiefs

Hillsborough has beaten off stiff competition to scoop the top prize at the annual 'Town Most Up Its Own Hole' awards, organised by the Northern Ireland Tourist Board.

The town was a 'clear winner' according to head judge Grant Causeway. 'We have very strict criteria for the competition,' he told us. 'Entrants must a) have a high number of resident dickheads, b) seem to think they're in England and c) be full of stuff that no one really likes but is a bit fancy – such as farmers' markets, overpriced restaurants and shops selling useless futtery shite made out of gingham.

'Hillsborough ticks all these boxes,' he continued, 'with the additional bonus of having an annual Oyster Festival. I mean, who the f**k even likes oysters, never mind organises an entire festival around them in a town miles from the sea? Folk in a town that's up its own hole, that's who.'

We sent our reporters onto the streets of town to see how the locals – or Hillsboroughtonians as they like to be known – felt about the award, and got a mixed reaction.

Solicitor Cameron Davidson told us it was wonderful news. 'This is wonderful news,' he said, as he queued in the chip shop for his lobster supper with white wine jus. 'Folk round here have been up their own holes for years. I personally have been up mine since I was twelve, so it's nice to get some recognition at last.'

Fancy cake shop owner Hermione Polopony was less keen.

'I'm worried it might be bad for business,' she told us. 'All kinds of riff raff might come into town to look at us and buy things in my lovely cake shop. This would stop me chatting with my lovely, lovely friends.'

However Finlay Finlayson, who has represented the Garden Party on the local council for twenty years, was more enthusiastic. 'It's the best thing to happen to the town since a Hillsborough side came third in the NI Poshest Bastards Championships of 1974, and I should know: I was the poshest bastard on the team.'

The North Down town of Holywood, described by the judges as 'a traffic jam with a maypole' came second, with close neighbours Crawfordsburn a distant third.

'Marchopoly' board game launched for Twelfth parades

Top US toy manufacturer Hasbro has unveiled a new version of its iconic board game Monopoly set in Northern Ireland during the marching season. Marchopoly will see players make their way round a board crowded with contentious locations, as they attempt to gather more grant funding and territory than themuns.

'We're sure that families will love the tweaks we've made to an old favourite,' says the game's designer Walter Cannon. 'We've changed all the locations, of course, and now you're trying to take over entire areas by building little green and orange houses and sticking flags on them.'

The traditional playing pieces have also been given a twist. The top hat has been replaced with a bowler hat, the car with a police Land Rover, and you can choose between a left and right boot, depending on which foot you kick with. Community Chest and Chance become Community Worker Chest and Chancers, with new cards that can provide either help or hindrance.

'Players should recognise them from the old game,' says Cannon. 'You have won second prize in a band contest – collect a £10 grant from each marcher, Advance to Grosvenor Road Police Station and go back three decades. There's still a Get out of Jail Free card, of course, but it's been supplemented by an On the Run letter.'

If the game does well in the toyshops we can expect to see more Northern Ireland-themed games, such as an Ulster-Scots version of Scrabble in which players have to spell words incorrectly, and Tiocfaidh-Roo, where you try to dangle things from Gerry Adams before he kicks them all off, denying everything.

Nazi flag offenders sentenced to eighteen months of History Channel

Police in Carrickfergus have charged a group of local men with twenty-seven counts of 'not having a f**king clue' after the appearance of several Nazi flags in the town, often on the same lamp post as the union flag.

In court this morning their defence team told the jury how their clients had 'naively' thought the aim of being a good honest sectarian was to put up 'loads of flags that offended themuns'.

However the prosecution later made mincemeat of this argument, visually explaining the nonsensical notion of supporting both the Nazis and the British, using a range of He-Man figures and a plastic replica of Castle Greyskull.

'So you see,' said QC John Battlecat, 'Royalists cannot support both Adam Prince of Eternia and Skeletor. It's just not possible.'

Passing sentence, Judge Philip Banks told the men that they 'needed a good boot up the hole', before ordering them to serve eighteenth months watching the History Channel.

BBC to introduce Glastonbury-style coverage for Twelfth parades

In a sensational move guaranteed to please music fans the world over, the BBC has announced that it intends to cover this year's Twelfth in the same detail as it covers the Glastonbury Festival.

'The BBC is committed to bringing its viewers the best in music,' said producer Fred Zeppelin, 'and the Twelfth is one of the biggest world music festivals around. We'll be covering all the main parades in the same way as we do Glastonbury – you'll be able to access them all through the red button on your remote control.'

'Our cameras will be everywhere, from the Eleventh Night bonfires right through to the Black parade at Scarva,' he explained. 'It's very similar to Glastonbury in many ways – three days and nights of people standing around in the rain whilst listening to obscure music and getting off their tits.'

Veteran presenter Jo Wylie is also enthusiastic. 'I'm really looking forward to interviewing some of the bands,' she told us. 'The variety of music is incredible – you have flute bands, accordions, more flute bands, Lambegs, other flute bands, bagpipes and even bigger flute bands.'

'It's not often that you get to meet your heroes,' she continued, 'so the opportunity to ask the bass drummer from Downshire Guiding Star about his musical influences is not to be missed, and I get to make the traditional BBC joke about who won the Sham Fight.'

Orange spokesman Schomberg Carson told us that the Order was delighted with the move. 'We've rebranded as "Orangefest" recently, but to be honest that's been a bit shit. It's really just facepainters and a bouncy castle for children whilst spides drink Buckfast. Maybe next year we'll have "Orangebury" and persuade the Foo Fighters to lead the parade in Fermanagh.'

In other news, Channel 4 staff have revealed that they intend to form a residents group, and will protest against the BBC coverage by showing three days of back-to-back episodes of *The Big Bang Theory*. 'No change there then,' said a representative of the station.

❝ The variety of music is incredible – you have flute bands, accordions, more flute bands, Lambegs, other flute bands, bagpipes and even bigger flute bands, ❞ Jo Wylie told us.

Belfast flooded with shellfish after politicians accidentally appeal for clams

Northern Ireland is suffering from a plague of molluscs after the First and Deputy First Ministers inadvertently issued a press release appealing for clams over the marching season.

It is understood that their request was relayed to God, who took it at face value and added millions of shellfish to the perpetual rain that has been falling across the country. As a result many parts of Belfast are now knee deep in the creatures, making driving conditions hazardous.

Despite the error there are hopes that the over-abundance of crustaceans may act as a deterrent to violence. 'It's hard to riot when you're up to your bollocks in molluscs,' said PSNI spokesman John Dory.

This is not the first time that seafood-related spelling mistakes have caused problems over the marching season. In 2006, Loyalists erecting an Eleventh Night bonfire had their event ruined when they took delivery of fivehundred wooden pollocks, a situation made worse by the fact that they'd also accidentally ordered a bouncy catfish and a plaice-fainter for the accompanying family fun day.

However all these incidents pale into insignificance compared to the red faces at PSNI headquarters in 2012 that followed the deployment of the Riot Squid to deal with trouble in North Belfast.

In related news, a number of other bad jokes involving the Orange Chowder, PIRAnha Fish, Ceremonial Swordfish, Stickiebacks and Trouts Being Shat failed to make this story.

> ❛ It's hard to riot when you're up to your bollocks in molluscs, ❜ said PSNI spokesman John Dory.

Government reveals plans for purpose-built parading stadium

After yet more appalling scenes in North Belfast last night, the British government has brought forward plans to construct a new eighty-thousand-seater stadium in the Titanic Quarter – designed specifically to host controversial Orange parades.

'Aye, we've been thinking about this for some time,' said NIO spokesman Herbert Blowin. 'Every year thousands of people enjoy themselves peacefully at Twelfth parades around the country, but in Belfast they all go clean buck mental. It's costing us hundreds of millions of pounds to police these things so we may as well spend the same money on something useful.'

It is understood that the new £250-million arena will have a specially designed 'marching track', complete with puddles, traffic lights and manholes, and will include a replica Catholic church outside which bandsmen can play whatever shite they want or around which they can dance, looking completely ridiculous. Close to the church an 'away end' will allow travelling fans to be offended to their heart's content, and a media section will be provided for press who like to gather at flashpoints.

A number of bars, shops and businesses will operate within the stadium, but these will close on parade days to replicate the city centre atmosphere. Instead, a range of crap fast-food outlets will serve traditional Twelfth fodder like half-cooked burgers,

and off-licences will sell only Buckfast and White Lightning cider. Whilst many stadia have FanZones outside the arena, the new 'Parade Ground' will instead have a RiotZone, where the two sides can buck plastic bricks and foam bottles at each other over a twenty-foot-wide trench in front of a mural depicting the Ardoyne shops.

Speaking through a megaphone, the Order's Belfast Master George Shitkick gave a guarded welcome to the proposals. 'We know that everyone is getting sick of watching a shar of drunken arseholes chucking stuff at the police in North Belfast, but unless an additional £250 million is spent on an exact replica of our traditional route, including a Twaddell camp, we'll reject it. This plan is typical of the lack of investment in Loyalist areas. All they do is waste money on policing our riots.'

Ardoyne resident Phelim O'Croissánt was also cautious. 'We spend all our days off hanging around in front of the shops – we'll have to be bussed down there every bank holiday just in case there's a parade to be offended by.'

As the news became public, rioting immediately started in Derry. 'Themuns in Belfast get everything,' said local hood Flapjack Doherty. 'I'm away to burn an Arts Centre because I think it's the Apprentice Boys' Hall.'

Ryanair begin charging customers to look out the window

Famously frugal airline Ryanair have announced their latest money-spinning innovation – charging passengers to look out the window.

The new system will now be rolled out across the entire European fleet 'within days'. Ryanair confirmed that passengers are able to gawk out the window for a good 'two to three minutes' simply by inserting a Euro into the coin slot provided.

As expected the announcement got a mixed reaction from passengers at Dublin airport today. 'I didn't really mind it as I slept most of the way,' said Sligo man, Seamus Emirates. 'But I do enjoy seeing the plane coming into land,

so I spent 6 euro on watching that. It's just as well I broke that €20 to buy two tiny cans of Heineken, to be honest. The leftover change was just perfect.'

However, not all travellers have seen the positive side. 'It was awful flying into Stockholm,' complained Derry woman, Maureen Etihad. 'All the nice views were on the right and so everyone on that side was firing euros in for about an hour. Then suddenly the plane lurched to the side and started going into a tailspin with the extra weight. The pilot eventually righted it and managed a bumpy landing but, Jaysus, it was scary biccies.'

Ryanair have famously made tens of millions in recent years by applying levies on everything imaginable, including excess luggage, overweight kids, in-flight vomiting and folk doing really smelly shites. This new initiative takes these charges a step further.

Company spokesman Gerry Lufthansa said, 'The system is all sorted now and it's entirely optional for passengers. It's just a bit of fun really. Like having your own arcade machine at your seat.' However he refused to be drawn on speculation that any Tampax and condom machines in their toilets would be replaced with spare-change machines for breaking notes.

Strabane offers to bail out cash-strapped Greece

Despite being labelled one of the most deprived areas of Northern Ireland, Strabane has made an audacious bid to improve its global economic reputation – by offering Greece a lend.

'Aye, we had a look at our finances, then we had a look at Greece's, and we realised that things weren't that bad after all,' said Noel Cash from Strabane Chamber of Commerce. 'So we got together and decided we'd like to help out by offering them a crisis loan. Turns out we're rich beyond their wildest dreams.'

Citizens across Greece are reportedly spending hours every day queuing at bank machines in an effort to withdraw their life savings for fear their banking system will collapse. 'Aye, we heard about that and felt lousy on them,' continued Cash, 'cos we've got loads of bank machines in Strabane that hardly anyone ever uses. So we decided,

feck it – we'll send our unused ATMs out there if they'll swap us a few of their fancy buildings.

'The Blue Parrot bar has called dibs on the Acropolis for a big comeback, and we reckon the Temple of Athena will make a quare snazzy bus station. Sure we'll not know ourselves!'

As part of the deal, The Ulster Fry understands that the world-famous Asda, Strabane, will be relocated to Greece as part of the financial-aid package. 'Aye, it's got loads of spare bank machines and

it's only really Derry wans that shop there, so we're happy to get shot of it, tbh,' he added finally. 'Besides, they are giving us Zeus in return.'

It is understood that the Greek god will use his lightning bolts to power the town's electricity supply for the foreseeable future, saving the town millions in household bills whilst Greece gets its act together.

Rumours that he would be played by Liam Neeson and arrive pre-fitted with a 'Pay & Go' meter remain unconfirmed at the time of going to press.

Northern Ireland to get its own budget airline

Following years of success for southern Irish flight providers Aer Lingus and Ryanair, a consortium of Northern Irish businessmen have set up their own rival airline in a bid to capitalise on growing a trend amongst local people for 'going places' and 'doing stuff'.

BeezerJet will launch in 2016, with several new routes to some of the most sought-after locations in the entire world for Northern Irish people. Passengers will thus be able to fly to a range of far-off exotic destinations, including Spain, Portugal, Scotland and Fermanagh.

'Ulster holidaymakers will soon be able to find flights based on criteria that really matter,' announced BeezerJet CEO, Hans Luggage, 'such as how cheap the fegs are, the stock levels of them humongous plastic bottles of sambuca in local supermarkets, and the availability of Sky Sports in pubs near your hotel.'

'Also, the BeezerJet website will be the first in the world with a "Payback Calculator" feature,' explained Luggage, 'which will quickly tell you how many cartons of fegs you need to bring back to cover the cost of your trip! We've worked tirelessly to secure deals with some of Europe's cheapest feg-selling regions and cost-effective places you've never heard of!'

The tailor-made Ulster offering doesn't end there.

'We've eradicated the baggage restrictions for lady travellers,' he continued. 'Turns out Norn Iron women have loads of baggage, so taking a leaf from society's book, we're letting them away with it, and making men pay the price for it instead.' However this claim was contested by The Ulster Fry Writers' Girlfriends' Union, who – it is reported – later punched their boyfriends in the arm and refused to put out for a week.

Early technical problems with the new website have been resolved after fears they would delay the airline's launch. 'Aye, people found the first version of our website far too easy to use and navigate,' admitted Luggage. 'Thankfully, though, we've been able to fix it by adding loads of annoying hidden options, insurance add-ons and confusingly worded opt-in/out tick-boxes, that make the process a proper pain in the hole.'

BeezerJet will launch in January 2016, with daily services from both the Calum Best International Airport and the Nadine Coyle Space Station.

> 'We've worked tirelessly to secure deals with some of Europe's cheapest feg-selling regions.'

Last non-tattooed man in Belfast 'to be captured and put on display in Ulster Museum'

The search has begun for the last remaining untattooed man in Belfast after a study carried out by Ballylumford University revealed that virtually everyone in the city now has some kind of body art. This has led to fears that in fifty years time children will have forgotten what it's like to have unadorned skin.

'Tattoos were once the preserve of sailors, bikers and ex-cons,' said Professor Walter Anchor of the university's anthropology department. 'But now everyone has them, regardless of age, sex or creed. It used to be thought a disadvantage for a candidate to have tatts on display in a job interview, but now you can bet one of the panel will have Love and Hate inked onto their knuckles, at the very least. I attended one recently where the interviewer had a full-face spider web, and showed me a dolphin on his arse after we shook hands.'

Professor Anchor told us that one of the most common tattoo forms he saw during the survey was the 'full sleeve' of ethnic art. 'Gone are the days of Mum and Dad on the forearm. We now expect to see entire left arms plastered in Polynesian symbolism. It must have some deep inner significance for people growing up in Bangor.'

The decision to hunt down the last 'unillustrated man' in the city was taken after the First and Deputy First Ministers revealed their tattoos at a recent press briefing. 'Arlene has a list of demands regarding Welfare Reform on her left arm,' says Professor Anchor, 'and Marty has "F**k you Arlene" etched on his chest.'

'Their inkings are beautifully symbolic of their relationship, but made us realise that if these two had them, we had to make a move or we'd lose touch with our natural state.'

It is understood that police are using specially trained uninked-skin-sniffing dogs to carry out searches for the final untattooed man. 'We won't shoot him or anything,' the professor told us. 'We'll just sedate him and stick him in a glass box in the museum foyer. Then when he dies we'll have him stuffed.'

NI motorists slam 'direction-pointing device' plan for cars

Northern Irish motorists have reacted angrily to plans drawn up by the Department of the Environment to introduce some kind of direction-pointing thing to all road vehicles.

Launching the scheme in a pizza shop this afternoon, DOE Minister Mark Hotsauce Durkan said the plan was part of a wide-ranging scheme to reform driving in the Province. 'It seems that most cars in Northern Ireland have no way of showing when they intend to pull in or overtake,' said the minister. 'We want to launch a consultation process to see if anyone can invent a device that would allow us to communicate our driving intentions to other road users.'

It is understood that the Department's favoured idea is a couple of orange lights fitted to each side of the front and rear of the vehicle. Under the radical scheme, motorists would be required to somehow flick these lights on to indicate which direction they intended to take when undergoing any manoeuvre, perhaps using switches attached to the steering column.

'This is an outrageous proposal,' said Audi Murphy, a particularly angry motorist from Magherafelt. 'It is every driver's God given right to turn randomly and overtake at will. If anything, these highfalutin indication devices will make roads much more dangerous.'

He was backed by Scania O'Toole, Chair of the Irish National Lorry Alliance. 'This is ridiculous,' he said. 'Are you telling me I'll have to flick some kind of switch every time I pull off into a lay-by so that I can pull off in a lay-by? It's political correctness gone mad.'

However Minister Durkan is adamant that the plan will be forced through the executive. 'If successful, this could be the start of a major overhaul of motoring in Northern Ireland,' he claimed. 'Before you know it, folk will be using headlights in poor driving conditions, taking the correct lanes at roundabouts, not driving up other folk's holes – the lot.'

When asked if the law would extend to farmers, taxi drivers and BMW owners, the minister was less certain. 'We can only go so far,' he told us, 'and extending the scheme to those motorists might be pushing it.'

Famous cranes 'Samson and Goliath' come out as gay

With Belfast's Pride Festival well underway, the two cranes that dominate the Belfast skyline have sensationally revealed that they are in a 'happy, consenting adult relationship', or as one observer put it, 'pure bucking the life out of each other'.

Goliath, who first arrived in Belfast in 1969, told us, 'The early years were lonely for me, but when Samson arrived in '73 I finally had some company. We started out friends, but after years of watching him sliding up and down my dock I eventually admitted the truth – that I had feelings for him.'

Samson too felt an early attraction. 'We were both interested in similar things, such as boats, lifting dead-heavy stuff and the colour yellow. It was uncanny! I remember looking at him across the harbour one day and realising how handsome he was. I used to just find myself gazing at him for hours. One day he actually caught me staring at him whilst he was taking a ship. #awkward!'

Like many relationships, though, the cranes have had problems. 'Aye, we've had lots and lots of ups and downs between us through the years,' revealed Goliath. 'We'd be really close one day, but we'd wake up the next to find we'd somehow drifted apart. For some reason big stuff has always tried to come between us, but when it does we just work through it together. A problem shared is a problem halved.'

The DUP reacted furiously to the news, though, insisting that the cranes should no longer be allowed to donate blood, bake cakes or get married. They've also called their biblical names into question. 'It's an affront to the good book to have these sodomites call themselves Samson and Goliath,' said DUP spokesman Alister Redface. 'We demand their first names be changed to something more suitable for two Cranes. Like Frasier and Niles.'

However Harland & Wolff spokesman Ali Minium congratulated the pair saying, 'We should have seen the signs sooner, really. They are the most outrageously fabulous couple on Queen's Island after all.'

> The DUP reacted furiously to the news, insisting that the cranes should no longer be allowed to donate blood, bake cakes or get married.

'Don't you mean Londonderry?' wins Best Joke Award at Edinburgh Fringe Festival

A Belfast man who made an original witty retort to some people he'd never met before has won the Best Joke Award at this year's Edinburgh Fringe Festival.

Lee Robinson from Belfast told us, 'I was in Edinburgh for the weekend with the missus when we bumped into a group of lads from up the country. We got chatting and I asked them where they were from. One said he was from Dungiven, another from Strabane and the last fella said, "Derry".

'Just then I had a flash of inspiration. I thought to myself, Jaysus, I can make my response educational, historically relevant, patronising and hilarious ... all at the same time. And then out of nowhere, I just blurted out, "Don't

you mean Londonderry?" It was pure class. Everyone fell about laughing. It wasn't awkward in the slightest and I didn't come across as passive-aggressive sectarian douchebag or anything.'

The joke beat off tough competition from an assortment of other cracking one-liners including, 'Did you do that wanking?' to a man wearing a bandage on his arm; 'Oh, watch out for the ladyboys' to a punter who was headed to Thailand on his honeymoon; and 'It's a great day for ducks' to anyone who'd listen after it started raining.

'It's been the most original and witty selection of ad-lib comedy we've ever seen here at the festival. Those responsible should be proud

of themselves,' said a spokesman. However the comedian behind the second-placed joke – 'Don't you mean Derry?' – has formally complained to festival organisers about being overlooked for someone from Belfast.

Meanwhile a group of local women who cut their hair to compete in the Fringe Festival have given the experience an extremely bad review on TripAdvisor. 'Load of shite,' wrote Imelda Wigwam. 'Not one person even approached us about our lovely new hairdos.'

Scouts will be shot, warns Boys' Brigade

Following mature and insightful commentary from local political 'expert' Jude Collins, who claimed that the Boys' Brigade are similar to local paramilitaries, Northern Ireland's worst fears have been realised as the country's two leading outdoor youth organisations declared war upon each other.

The Boys' Brigade made the first move in the offensive, unveiling an orienteering course in Crawfordsburn Country Park which leads to a 'Scouts will be shot' message written in twigs and branches at the end. The PSNI have confirmed that the threat is real, and that they found a cache of air rifles hidden in little Billy's rucksack, which they say 'might have put someone's eye out'.

Local scouts took no time in

retaliating, however, dispensing a punishment beating to two Boys' Brigade members who slagged off their knots and critiqued their tent pitching skills. The Mater Hospital have confirmed they are now treating two 9-year-olds for Chinese burns, two dead arms, severe diddy nips and a suspected wedgie.

Local paramilitaries have vowed to keep their communities safe from the emerging threat of 'outdoor activists' – and have banned anyone from making campfires in their area smaller than forty feet high. 'We urge residents to remain vigilant and to contact their local numbskull if they spot anyone starting a fire without the correct equipment – such as pallets, tractor tyres and a gallon of petrol.'

It is understood that delegations

from the Boys' Brigade and Scouting Ireland have since been brought together for peace talks with leading political parties. The DUP has refused to attend after learning that they had to make camp first.

One source has described the negotiations as being 'in tents'.

Mr Collins has since been awarded his Excavation Merit Badge for his follow-up appearance on *Nolan Live* last night. 'Not only is he an ageing fossil,' remarked one viewer, 'but he dug a quare f**king hole for himself.'

Celeb chefs ready to cook up a storm for Ulster customers

Fans of gourmet food in Northern Ireland are salivating this evening after it emerged that several top chefs are to follow the example of Marco Pierre White and open restaurants here.

The news that the French gastronome is to open an eatery in East Belfast's salubrious Park Avenue Hotel was swiftly followed by an announcement that housewife's favourite Jamie Oliver is to take over the hot food counter at Jamesie's Centra at the foot of the Glenshane Pass.

'The name just fits perfectly,' the Naked Chef told us. 'We'll be serving veggie roll, Scotch eggs, jambons, the lot. I know it doesn't fit well with all that healthy school dinners bullshit I used to come out with, but six sausage rolls for two quid? You couldn't beat that.

'It'll be pukka,' he added. 'Whatever that means.'

Meanwhile Gordon Ramsay is to trade in his Hell's Kitchen for an ice cream van with a pitch on the scenic North Antrim Coast. 'It'll be f**king class,' the foul-mouthed chef told reporters. 'Not everyone likes that fancy muck I make, but who doesn't like a nice poke on a Sunday?

'I'll mostly be setting up in Portrush through the summer, but during the winter I'll take a rake round the local schools and sell the kids single fags,' he concluded, before swearing a lot and punching a photographer.

Fish enthusiast Rick Stein has followed suit and plans to take over the doughnut stand in the car park of the Derry branch of TK Maxx. 'No one eats any of that fish shite I make anyway,' he told us, 'and this is a cash business. Do you think the taxman will have a clue how many doughnuts I sell? Will he f**k … it's a licence to print money.'

Not everyone has welcomed the news. Local celebrity chefs Paul Rankin and Jenny Bristow held a joint press conference this afternoon at which they told journalists they would 'not stand idly by and allow foreign chefs to steal our customers'.

'At this stage we plan only peaceful protests,' said Rankin, 'though we cannot rule out an armed response.'

'Sprouts will be shat,' added Bristow.

> Jamie Oliver to take over the hot food counter at Jamesie's Centra.

Men wearing shorts to work in danger of getting 'a good boot up the hole', warns PSNI

The Police Service of Northern Ireland has warned men considering wearing shorts to the office tomorrow that they could be in for a 'whole handlin' – possibly leading to a 'wile kickin'.

The caution comes after a morning of 'horrendous' pale-hairy-leg flaunting across the Province, which has seen over 73 per cent of men arrive to work in what can only be described as a baggy-combat-shorts-with-flip-flops combination. Or as one fashion expert said, 'f**king wile-looking'.

It is understood that trouble flared in Belfast after several men took their footwear off to walk around in their bare feet, forcing traumatised colleagues to take early retirement. There are also reports that one meeting at the InvestNI offices got 'out of hand' when some boy arrived late, on a surfboard.

'The law is quite clear on this,' explained top cop Barry Billabong. 'Shorts are reserved for outdoor stuff, sports and going on holiday. But these boys who think they can wear beachwear to the office now cos it hasn't rained for a couple of days need a good boot up the hole – and our intelligence indicates that they are gonna get one.'

Raising the threat level to 'amber', the PSNI have warned NI males not to wear shorts to work tomorrow 'unless you're a footballer' and only to wear sandals 'if you are Jesus'.

In other unrelated sports news, Ards Football Club have announced that tomorrow's morning training session will be played in jeans and sensible shoes.

Middle-aged men 'fed up with being ogled by young women'

With the good weather finally allowing us to shed our winter clothes, middle-aged men up and down the country are complaining of being 'treated like pieces of meat' by younger women, according to a report released today.

Commissioned by the Northern Ireland Men's Liberation Front, the report reveals that leering women are making their male counterparts feel uncomfortable as they attempt to relax in the sunshine. We sent our reporters out on the streets of Belfast to see just how widespread the problem is.

'I should be able to dress how I see fit,' said 46-year-old Barry Tubbs. 'If I want to leave a couple of buttons undone on my shirt or strip down to my vest, I'm doing it because I'm feeling hot, not because I want to look hot. I really don't need these young dolls trying to get a glimpse down my top. It's my body after all.'

'Aye, they're all at it,' said bank clerk Simon Chunker, who we found relaxing outside the City Hall. 'Look at them. I'm just trying to enjoy my lunch in the sunshine and they're all sitting there in their little strappy tops, undressing me with their eyes. It demeans me as a man.'

51-year-old Sean Bloat had much the same complaint. 'I decided to wear shorts today, and have regretted it ever since,' he told us. 'Admittedly they've seen better days and are a bit tight round the sheugh, but I should be able to go for a slider without some wee cutty ogling my arse-cleavage at the poke van.'

We decided to approach some women for their opinion on the scandal, but when we asked some random ladies if they enjoyed staring at scantily clad men in public places they immediately reported us to the police.

Inventive Belfast pub installs world's first fleg machine

With the elections looming and the marching season just around the corner, one Belfast pub has struck upon an ingenious way to make money from Northern Ireland's honest, hard-working sectarians – the world's first fleg machine.

For the first time ever, drunken city centre revellers can now get off their faces whilst simultaneously getting into other people's faces, simply by choosing their fleg of choice, priced at a reasonable £5.20, from Northern Ireland's newest vending-machine innovation – FlegOMatic.

Bar manager Albie Grand told us, 'With this new machine we are finally able to offer our customers what they really want at an affordable price. Sure people come in here to buy beer, cocktails and all that shite, but once they've a couple of drinks in them, you know the craic – everyone starts gasping for a fleg! Thanks to the machine, we now offer our customers a wide variety of flegs to suit a range of tastes and occasions.'

Concerned about the health risks of flowing flegs in other peoples faces indoors, however, Health Minister Jim Wells took a break from insulting gay folk to insist that the bar install a special outside flegging area – where people can go and enjoy a fleg in the fresh air.

'Aye, I think it's a really good idea,' said customer Lambeg Johnston. 'I bought myself a new Norn Iron fleg there. Its nice to come out here and flow it into the night air in peace.'

Not everyone was so positive. 'I tapped a spare fleg off someone earlier, but it was revolting,' admitted Dissident O'Hagan. 'I was pure dying for a fleg, like, but when I put it up, I realised it was a feckin Union Jack. Boke.'

Whilst management admitted some minor riots had already broken out in the area, they have now installed signs warning customers not to tap flegs, whilst reminding patrons of the dangers that second-hand flegs can cause.

As we left, we spoke to one lopsided customer who told us he was still 'sussing out' the new fleg machine. 'I've put about a hundred quid into the bastard so far and it still hasn't paid out,' said Danny Accumulator. 'I'm just waiting on three of a kind,' he added, before ordering another pint of Aftershock.

> For the first time ever, drunken city centre revellers can now get off their faces whilst simultaneously getting into other people's faces, simply by choosing their fleg of choice.

The people of Northern Ireland were left stunned yesterday when they learned that more than fifty trainee officers had been found cheating in their police exams. That got us thinking about how hard this test must be, so we sent our best undercover reporter to the training college.

After he successfully scraped through the rigorous 50/50 recruiting policy by pretending to be one of themuns, he managed to nick some of the questions which we have reproduced for you here.

Answers at the bottom of the page.

PSNI EXAM QUESTIONS

(1) There are four of you in the Land Rover and the sergeant sends you into Costa for some doughnuts. How many do you buy?

_____

(2) A crime is reported at 18.03. You are ten minutes away by car, but you're on a bike. When do you arrive to investigate?

_____

(3) You're called to give evidence at a policing board meeting. What key points do you need to cover?

_____

(4) You are in a dance competition against PSNI Craigavon. Why?

_____

(5) You are travelling at a speed of 20 mph and Gerry Kelly leaps out of nowhere onto your bonnet. What do you do?

_____

(6) If the average police officer earns £30,000 a year, and the PSNI say it costs £24,000 per day to police the Twaddell Camp, how many officers are at Twaddell every day?

_____

(7) Robert, Trevor and Sean are in the back of the Land Rover. Robert gets out and Declan gets in. Factoring that Declan is left handed and that water cannons require need two people to operate them, how many cups of coffee should the driver ask the girl at McDonalds drive-thru window for?

_____

(8) There is a bit of trouble at the play park. One of the kids has cut his knee – how should you comfort him?

_____

ANSWERS
1. Eight, one each for now, one each for afters.
2. Wednesday.
3. Your back and your arse.
4. Because dance is the best way to get down with the kids. Just ask Brucie.
5. Ask him for a promotion.
6. Who cares? Think of the overtime!
7. Five. You forgot about Big Dave in the passenger seat.
8. Show him your pepper spray.

HOW DID YOU SCORE?
1–3 Civvy street.

4–6 Well done! Riot squad for you.

7–8 Did you cheat? Don't worry – we'll give you another crack and you can try to do worse next time.

'Balakinis' to be issued on Northern Irish beaches

Following the news that French authorities are forcing Burkini-wearing women to strip off, local councils in Northern Ireland have also released guidelines for how people should dress on their beaches.

However the authorities here are turning the French plan on its head and demanding that all visitors cover up as much as possible by wearing a Balakini – a combination of a wetsuit and full face balaclava that they claim is the only way to be fully protected from the elements.

'Let's face it,' said Cecilia One-Piece, Portrush's new community safety officer. 'It's f**king freezing on our beaches. Only an idiot would wear anything less than five layers. Despite this, we're seeing loads of wee hussies turning up here with their baps on show, or wee eejits going "taps aff". It's enough to give you goosebumps.'

The councils began patrolling some of our most popular beaches this morning issuing Balakinis to any underdressed holidaymakers.

Needless to say, the patrols met with a mixed reaction, with one American visitor we found on Portstewart Strand objecting strongly to being forced to wear the outfit. 'It's my God-given right to wear whatever I want to the beach,' said 48-year-old Buddy Smuggler, as he huddled beneath a blanket looking for his testicles.

However his partner Attracta Wheel-Nut was more enthusiastic. 'Sure a balaclava's quite traditional in Ireland isn't it?' she told us, 'and it's better than looking at his fat face anyway.'

The councils have also received support from the French government, who are said to be delighted to learn that another country has decided to make a complete dick of itself by issuing laws about what you can and can't wear on the beach.

'It's zee way we do things en France,' explained President François Hollande, 'Liberté, égalité, conformité, or whatever that auld shite is.'

> ❛ It's f**king freezing on our beaches. Only an idiot would wear anything less than five layers, ❜ said Cecilia One-Piece.

ATTENTION PARENTS: IT IS NATIONAL STAND IN FRONT OF A DOOR IN YOUR SCHOOL UNIFORM WEEK

PARENTS NOT UPLOADING PHOTOS TO FACEBOOK MAY BE PROSECUTED

(Fridges and fireplaces also allowed)

YEEOOODA

FLEGGS

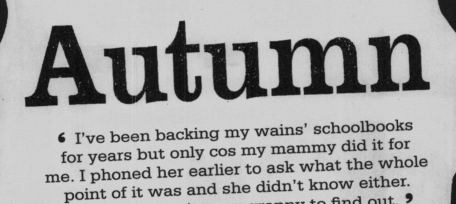

Autumn

'I've been backing my wains' schoolbooks for years but only cos my mammy did it for me. I phoned her earlier to ask what the whole point of it was and she didn't know either. She's away to ring my granny to find out.'

Enormous spiders now eligible for housing benefit

With domestic spiders reaching mammoth proportions, the Tories have had to face the fact that millions of gigantic arachnids will soon qualify for housing benefit under their recent welfare reforms.

'At first we thought, brilliant – they are big and ugly enough to pay rent now. But then we realised the creepy bastards are all unemployed layabouts and that we'd have to foot the bill for the big f**kers ourselves. And have you seen how many feet they have?'

Scientists claim the humongous spiders arrived on the wind from abroad but this is disputed by local spider Paddy Crawley, a father of 125 living in Bangor. 'We took the bus up from Strabane,' he explained. 'Me and herself climbed into a big

GAA bag for a dirty weekend and ended up here. We decided to move in and have wains. They're upstairs playing there, taking turns standing in the bath 'til someone comes in and screams. It's wile craic altogether.'

The government is now hurriedly trying to get the creatures ready for workplace employment but it's a huge task according to our source. 'We tried them as cleaners to start with,' said Ted Backwash from the Department of Employment and Learning. 'They are great at getting into those hard to reach places, but once you show them a hoover, they run a feckin' mile.'

'Next we tried them as dishwashers,' he continued. 'They were okay with plates and cutlery, but if you go near them with a glass they freak out. And don't even get me started on their web design skills FFS.'

Despite this, many gigantic spiders have gone on to promising careers in sports entertainment. 'Aye, that big bastard under your sofa is training to become a WWE wrestler,' revealed Backwash. 'He's gonna be fighting Brock Lesnar in next year's Royal Rumble. There's a bit of an unfair weight advantage, obviously… but Brock is beating the weight gainer into him to catch up!'

❝ We took the bus up from Strabane, ❞ claims local spider Paddy Crawley, a father of 125.

Marketing mishap as NI farmers descend on Belfast for Culchie Night

Belfast is currently engulfed in rural drama after an arts council administrative error led to a mistake in the publicity material for Culture Night, leading thousands of country folk to believe that everyone in the Big Smoke was throwing a party for them.

Police were alerted to the Culchie Night mix-up after a cavalcade of tractors drove off the Westlink and proceeded to reverse-parallel-park into roadside parking bays around the city centre. 'Wan pound fifty til taytime. Jaysus, thon's quare 'n' steep sur!' said Donemanagh man Dawson Creek. 'Now, which way to this big shindig?' he added, as he excitedly spat in his hands and rubbed them together.

However it wasn't long before issues arose. 'Jays, some strange goings-on up this neck of the woods,' complained Ballyhalbert farmer John-Joe Johnston. ''Tis all folk gawking at paintings and reading a lock of poetry. What time will all the good-lukkin weemin be here at for an oul jive?'

Across Belfast's trendy Cathedral Quarter right now, red-faced men are growing even more red-faced, as security men 'luk down their noses at them' for not meeting the required dress code. 'We eventually got into that famous Belfast Muriel's place,' moaned welly-booted Lisnaskea man Ted Glenn. 'But there wasn't one gable wall covered in sectarian slogans anywhere. It was just a pile of silly hoors with big beards drinking ginger ale outta f**king jam jars.'

Around the corner at the Black Box, meanwhile, security staff had even more bother with their women folk, who believed the venue was some sort of national meeting place for feminists with a more casual approach to grooming their nether regions. Police were soon called to deal with a number of excited ladies ready to whip off their trousers to prove they were eligible to enter.

City folk reckon it's already the best Culture Night in years. 'We're just out of Mac Theatre,' revealed art fan Gemma Ducksauce, 'and they have put on the most fabulous check-shirt installation in their foyer using real actors. One of them even approached me and asked me if I was well,' she revealed, 'cos apparently I'm looking well.'

This is the second such mishap in recent years, of course. Hundreds of disappointed farmers famously descended on Derry's 'CulchieTECH' festival in 2013 expecting to gawk at innovative new muck-spreaders, hay-balers and yard-scrapers.

Peace Process under threat as dissidents switch to Samsung Note 7

There are growing concerns for peace and prosperity in Northern Ireland after reports emerged that dissident factions of both Republican and Loyalist terror groups have begun stockpiling the deadly Samsung Note 7.

The PSNI have started patrolling shopping centres across the Province following the news, in an attempt to ward off the threat of terrorists arming themselves at Carphone Warehouse.

'These deadly phones are a game changer,' admitted PSNI bomb disposal expert Sam Tex. 'Someone phoned a warning through last night saying they were putting a Note 7 outside a local police station. However the stupid hoor actually called us using the Note 7 so thankfully his plan blew up in his face … literally!'

'We're taking reports of the amount of damage our exploding handsets can cause very seriously' said Linus Crackley from Samsung. 'We're always striving to improve our products and it's clear we need to up our game.'

'So we're pleased to announce that the new "Samsung Barrack-Buster 8" will be ready in time for Christmas. It'll have eight times the explosive capability and comes with a free three-month subscription to Spotify.'

Not to be outdone rivals Apple have fast-tracked work on the iPhone7-C4, which experts say will introduce a revolutionary new 'Hand-Grenade Mode'.

However fanboys are unhappy with rumours that the tech giant plans to do away with the physical grenade pin in favour of a wireless bluetooth trigger.

'Pretentious f**king hipster grenades,' remarked one man we spoke to. 'Lovely design, though,' he added.

'It's very worrying,' admitted a senior government spokesman later. 'People haven't exploded on the phone like this since we hired Concentrix.'

Massive GAA bags exposed as secret cattle-smuggling operation

Relationships between town and country were put under strain this morning after it emerged that police have uncovered an ancient All-Ireland cattle-smuggling operation. The bust started innocently when police called to a student house in Belfast's Holylands area, asking the residents to turn down the volume on their thirty-seventh repeat-play of Garth Brooks' *Greatest Hits*. It is reported that neighbours had complained that 'tomorrow had already come' and they had to 'get up in three f**king hours'.

Once at the scene, however, one officer noticed that a ginormous bulging O'Neill's bag in the hallway was gently mooing, and quickly called in reinforcements. Four male housemates from Tyrone, Down, Fermanagh and Armagh were immediately

detained for questioning. They soon cracked under pressure and revealed that their cross-country, tracksuit-wearing, bag-hauling escapades were merely a front for Ireland's oldest inter-county cattle-rustling scam.

One of the detained, 23-year-old Paddy Cochran from Cookstown, admitted he'd only been pretending to study Advanced Carpet Mechanics at Queen's University, but had in fact been working as a mule for a beef cartel in Aughnacloy.

Another, Fearghal O'Rourke from Kilkeel, supposedly studying a Masters of the Universe, broke down and revealed that his local hurling team were merely stick-wielding enforcers for the Rostrevor Triads, who have been flooding the streets of Newry with black-market semi-skimmed milk.

The ingenious operation is

feared to have penetrated the entire country, with a network of sports-clad operatives illegally transporting livestock on Translink and Bus Éireann services throughout Ireland in colossal GAA bags.

A Department of Agriculture spokesman admitted the effectiveness of customs sniffer dogs was now in doubt after early tests showed that just a few pairs of sweaty O'Neill's socks could mask the scent of three heifers and fifty pounds of manure.

O'Neill's bag found mooing in hallway.

Jackie Fullerton's real reason for leaving the BBC

Football fans in Northern Ireland reacted with dismay when it emerged that veteran commentator Jackie Fullerton had been sensationally 'retired' by the BBC, just before the Euro 2016 finals.

However, The Ulster Fry has learned that this was in fact a calculated move by the legendary broadcaster, as he has an even more impressive job lined up – replacing Daniel Craig in the role of 007.

'Jackie has been considered for the role before,' said our source at Broadcasting House. 'When Roger Moore stepped aside, Jackie was being lined up to play Bond in *The Living Daylights*. His suave personality and ability to carry off a safari suit made him an ideal candidate, but sadly the producers opted for Timothy Dalton, and it took the movie franchise years to recover.'

Director Sam Mendes, who has been behind the camera for recent Bond outings, admitted that casting the 72-year-old football commentator would require a change in approach. 'Aye, Jackie is probably not as physically fit as Daniel Craig, so we'll have to cut out a lot of the running about that Bond gets up to. Mostly he'll just sit in a commentary box making astute observations on the work of some evil super-villain, whilst occasionally getting overexcited about a pass by Chris Brunt. We'll also have to lose Bond's trademark dinner suit and replace it with a well-cut sports jacket and a pair of Farah slacks, and exchange the "shaken not stirred" martini for a gin and Lilt.'

The Ulster Fry understands that Fullerton's first outing as Bond is slated for 2017, in a movie provisionally named *From Windsor Park With Love*.

> We'll exchange the 'shaken not stirred' martini for a gin and Lilt.

Getting drunk 'too complicated these days'

Hardened drinkers are becoming increasingly confused by the range of alcoholic beverages on offer in pubs and clubs, according to a report published today in local consumer magazine *Wha?*

The article claims that pub goers were more content when they were limited to a narrow range of beers, spirits and mixers rather than the plethora of bottles that now lurks behind the average bar. 'If you went to a pub in the 1980s or '90s, you could expect to see three or four draft offerings – perhaps Guinness, lager and cider – then your staple spirits on optic,' says the author of the report Dr Campari Spritzer. 'Nowadays you can hardly get served by staff that lurk behind the array of towering beer pumps that run the length of the bar.

'To these we must add craft beers and fruit ciders. Gone are the days when you'd just order a pint of cider or, if you were feeling exotic, a bottle of Magners with ice. Now you're offered summer fruits, strawberry with a hint of elderflower or kiwi fruit with a dash of seaweed. In my opinion, you can stick all that up your arse,' says Spritzer.

This, of course, relies on the ability of the drinker to actually get served in the first place, as inevitably there will be a queue of cocktail drinkers taking up the bar staff's time with ridiculously complicated orders.

'In many bars you'll be behind a load of beardy wankers and cackling women who are requesting tin buckets of ridiculously named drinks which they'll then sip from chipped tea cups,' continues Dr Spritzer. 'This leaves the average drinker queuing for twenty minutes, clutching a tenner as he waits to buy two pints of Guinness and a bag of Bacon Flavour Fries. It's time for separate queues at bars – one for normal folk and one for the craft-beer-swilling, flavoured-vodka-tasting, "aren't-cocktails-sophisticated?" types.'

The confusion is having an adverse effect on the bar trade. 'People aren't drinking at home because pubs are too expensive, they're doing it because they know they'll get served when they go into the kitchen and won't have to listen to a crowd of office workers who think they're hipsters talking shite about craft gins.'

We sent our reporter to Belfast's trendy Apartment Bar to get the opinion of the staff working there, but so far he has been unable to report back as he's still waiting to be served.

> The confusion is affecting trade.

New Belfast restaurant to serve food on plates

In what has been described as 'the most revolutionary development for a generation' a trendy new Belfast restaurant has decided to serve meals on things called plates.

Situated on the edge of the Cathedral Quarter, The Lazy Millbag has turned its back on traditional tableware like chopping boards, roof slates and tin buckets, opting instead for innovative items apparently collectively called crockery. 'We think that consumers in Belfast are ready for this move,' says owner Philip Stake. 'Most restaurants are more old fashioned. I've even been served a meal on a bin lid – I mean, how retro is that?'

'We've ordered in the latest in tableware from Japan,' he continued. 'They're just round pieces of china on which food can be placed, but we're hoping our customers will soon get used to them.'

Philip also intends to serve all of the food for each course on a single plate, rather than going for the usual collection of miniature plant pots, tiny chip-pan baskets and skillets. 'It's a radical form of presentation,' he told us, 'but we feel it makes the eating experience more enjoyable as the customer will actually have room on the table to set down their drink without fear of setting fire to themselves.'

In a further innovative move, diners will also be treated to the latest in restaurant furniture. 'We're all used to eating at old school desks or recycled work benches and sitting on a chairs made out of pallets,' Philip says, 'so I'm hoping our futuristic "tables and chairs" will add something to the eating experience.'

Restaurant critic Hugo Hamilton, from local style magazine *Le Ganch*, isn't so sure that the craze will take off. 'Diners in Belfast are very traditional,' he claims. 'We expect to be served our fish on a house brick and our drinks in a jam jar, and prefer to sit on bean bag chairs and eat off an old front door.'

Ulster Fry 'not bad for you', says Ulster Fry

A report published today by Northern Irish website The Ulster Fry has poured cold water on a different report also released today by the World Health Organisation (WHO).

According to the WHO document, processed meats are extremely bad for you, leading to an increased cancer risk if you consume more than 50g per day – the equivalent of one sausage or two slices of bacon.

However The Ulster Fry's report has utterly repudiated these claims. 'These items are key constituents of a balanced diet,' says chief researcher Denny Hull. 'Everyone knows that the five main food groups are bacon, sausages, eggs, soda bread and potato bread, although our nutritional experts also advise adding beer to this list in order to maintain a healthy lifestyle.'

'It's important to note that the word "beans" does not feature,' he continued. 'Adding beans to a fry is what makes it unhealthy, and we must have some standards.'

We put these claims to the head of the World Health Organisation Professor Killjoy Spoilsport. 'Aye, you're right,' he confessed. 'We must have missed out all that stuff you're talking about when we were doing our calculations.'

We then asked if he would admit that he had been talking out of his arse. 'Fair enough,' he replied. 'Everyone should have known our advice was bollocks as soon as they saw the bit about only eating one sausage a day. I mean, who has one sausage at a time? People making stuff up, that's who.'

Following the scandal the United Nations has announced that it will be abolishing the World Health Organisation. 'From now on we'll be getting The Ulster Fry to do all our research into food and stuff,' said Secretary-General Ban Ki-moon, at the launch of a new report entitled 'Beer is Class'.

Andy Carroll ruled out of medical treatment for four to six weeks due to fitness

Having spent most of last season impressing the club's medical staff with his never-say-die attitude to missing football matches, doctors and physios at West Ham United have been left reeling after a medical scan on the player revealed dangerously high levels of fitness in his system.

Following a second opinion from specialists at nearby Newham General hospital, the club's medical staff were forced to accept the loss of their star patient – who will now be unavailable for treatment room selection whilst he works to become fully unfit again.

In a statement West Ham boss Slaven Bilić confirmed, 'The physio team at West Ham United are naturally disappointed that a player of Andy Carroll's calibre has been sidelined from treatment whilst he undergoes a period of playing football.'

'The scans are pretty conclusive, though, so on doctors' orders, we've been forced to consider selecting him to play upfront against his old club Newcastle tonight whilst he continues his dehabilitation.'

It is expected that injury-prone Carroll will have to undergo several football match treatments before he's unfit enough to return to medical action. However the club is fairly optimistic that the Geordie hitman will be back on the treatment table in 'around four to six weeks'.

> Medical staff are facing the loss of their star patient.

Dissidents 'very close' to uniting Ireland, reveals poll

Following another bomb scare today, the orchestrators of recent security alerts around the Province have today spoken of their 'pride' at finally uniting Ireland in a single unifying belief.

'Our figures indicate that people here are approaching 99.98 per cent agreement that we're a bunch of f**king cretins,' revealed division commander Jim Hallion, a cunning military strategist who until now has evaded police detection by hiding in plain sight as an unemployed layabout.

'Once we get everyone behind a single idea, the plan is to start slowly changing their minds to suit our nefarious intentions. Or at least I think that's what they are,' he laughed. 'They said a lot

of cracker words in *Despicable Me*, it's wile hard to keep track.'

The unsuccessfulness of the current dissident terror campaign has been unparalleled in recent years. 'Aye, we estimate we've cost the PSNI tens of pounds worth of damage in thon yellow cordon-off tape,' he boasted. 'And sure if one of our poorly made

bombs manages to kill someone eventually, we'll just make more inroads on convincing the remaining 0.02 per cent of the population not to get behind us.'

The claims have been rejected by 99.98 per cent of the population, however, who insist they DO want get behind dissidents … but only to give them a good boot up the hole.

Hurricanes to be given proper scary names, says Met Office

As Storm Abigail wreaks its windy vengeance across Northern Ireland, the Met Office has finally admitted that giving storms girls' and boys' names is stupid.

The news comes less than a month after the weather-watching department announced a new list of names that would mean the next storm after Abigail would be called Barney, before a host of other names including Steve and Vernon. 'Aye, we've decided it's a bit childish,' confessed Met Office expert Michael Snow. 'The next gale we have could be destroying peoples' houses, all the while boasting the name of a big purple dinosaur.'

The department's new list of

names will still be alphabetical but will be more in tune with the havoc wreaked by such storms. 'First up after Abigail will be Hurricane Big Windy Bastard,' says Snow, 'and then we'll have Calamity Storm Bollocks. I'm sure you'll agree that's much more descriptive.'

A full list of the new storm titles is below. We understand that shortly after this list was published our Met Office expert Michael Snow was sacked.

Abigail

Big Windy Bastard

Calamity Storm Bollocks

David Cameron

Even Bigger Windy Bastard

Fartypants

Ganch

Hallion

I'll Stay Indoors Ye Hoorbeg

Jaysus It's Caul

Katie Hopkins

Loud Windy Stormy Fecker

Mister Windy Trousers

Nipple Pincher

Oul Hoor

Peter Robinson

Quare an' Windy

Rectal Thermometer

Shitehole

Toolbeg

Ugly Motherfecker

Very Ugly Motherfecker

Wanker

Xylophone

Yer Ma's Wind

Zebra Farts

ITV to move *Corrie* to Craigavon after UTV takeover

The Northern Irish media world was shaken to its very core today by the news that ITV is to buy local network UTV.

The news was swiftly followed by an even more earth-shattering announcement from the British TV giant – as executives revealed that as part of the plan they intend to relocate the popular soap *Coronation Street* to Northern Ireland.

'It makes sense financially as filming costs are much lower here,' said ITV insider Ken Duckworth. 'At first we considered Belfast, but then we discovered there was a real place called Coronation Street in Craigavon, so the location choice was practically made for us.'

Inevitably there will be changes to both the cast and the plot when the show crosses the Irish Sea. 'Regular viewers will have got used to Jim McDonald as the only Northern Irish character. Well, that's going to change,' says Duckworth. 'From now on there'll be only one token Englishman in the show – probably Ken Barlow – and everyone else will talk like Big Jim and say "so it is" all the time, so they will.'

Some well known settings will also change as a result of the move. 'We'll have to rename Roy's Rolls Roy's Baps,' we were told by the show's producer Emily Fairclough, 'and the Rovers Return is going to be taken over by the local paramilitaries, with ex-prisoner Winkie Nelson behind the bar.'

However, unlike the busy Rovers, the new bar will reflect the current NI economic climate and be deserted. 'Aye, people can't afford to drink in the bar all day in this day and age,' continued Fairclough, 'so we're replacing the Kabin with an offie as everyone will be drinking carry-outs at the house instead. We've even convinced a legendary cast member to come back and run it as Curley's Wine Cellar.'

The first episode of the new series will air next summer, with a plot focusing around Gail Platt's application for a bonfire grant, and a crisis as the Rosamund Street Residents' Collective prevent the Rising Sons of Stan Ogden returning from the Twelfth.

9 STAR WARS CHARACTERS FROM NORN IRON

YEEOOODA

Ancient Jedi Master Yeeoooda isn't the full shilling these days. 800 years of bating the Buckie into him have rotted his brain and he now talks in out of order gibberish and lives in a swamp in the old Antrim Road Waterworks. Give him odds you will, hmm.

PRINCESS LEIABOUT

After years of leading the rebellion, Princess Leiabout can't be arsed anymore. She has three wains who do her head in and she lies on the sofa smoking fegs and ordering groceries from Iceland's website. The Prime Minister of Iceland has now blocked her emails.

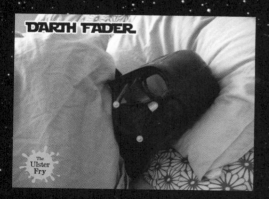

DARTH FADER

Whilst supposedly a mighty warrior who can party through the darkside of night, Darth Fader is actually notorious for slipping off to bed or falling asleep on the sofa with a half drunk can of beer. F**king lightweight.

JAM JAR DRINKS

After his unpopular appearance in The Phantom Menace, this floppy eared nuisance turned to the Dark n Stormy Side of the Force. He can now be found hanging around hipster bars sucking rum cocktails out of teapots, jam-jars and flower pots whilst talking absolute bollocks.

Secretary of State confirms that bears shit in the woods

The Secretary of State for Northern Ireland today told the House of Commons that paramilitaries here are still armed, and that their members are still 'up to shite'.

The shock revelations shocked nobody, with an estimated 95 per cent of the population bewildered that the issue was ever in question. 'You mean they were meant to have gone away?' was the incredulous reaction of most people, with the other 5 per cent pretending that they thought all the paramilitaries had retired and spent their time doing yoga.

Ms Villiers went on to state a number of other really f**king obvious things. 'The IMC have judged that the Pope is a member of the Catholic faith, and has been for some time,' she told MPs. 'They also believe that the nights are fair drawing in, Freddos have got more expensive and traffic isn't as heavy during the school holidays.'

Local politicians have reacted in their usual measured tones. 'This is bollocks,' said SF president Gerry Adams. 'The IRA disbanded ages ago and none of its members have had a shit in the woods in over ten years.' PUP leader Billy Hutchinson was similarly scathing. 'The UVF have been off the scene for some time,' he told us. 'All weapons were handed in and the former members have since devoted their lives to prayer and contemplation. Basically the UVF is now a kind of retirement organisation for Loyalist monks.'

Meanwhile Peter Robinson is going to be First Minister again, as now that the existence of the IRA has apparently been confirmed he feels that there is no need for his ministers to resign just in case the IRA exists.

'It doesn't make sense to me either,' he told journalists, 'but sure we're all just making it up as we go along.'

'The UVF is now a retirement organisation for loyalist monks,' claims the PUP.

The Ulster Fry

Channel 4 to add 'Norn Iron week' to *Bake Off*

As the world recovers from the shock news that *The Great British Bake Off* is to move from the BBC to Channel 4, it has emerged that a key selling point was the addition of a Northern Ireland-themed week.

'We wanted to move away from all that fancy muck like choux pastry and fairy cakes,' says show producer Carmel Square. 'Yousuns over there are famous for your range of bakery stuff, so we thought we'd give it a Viennese whirl, so to speak.'

Next year viewers will be treated to a full spread of Norn Iron products, with contestants expected to try their hands at everything from sausage roll baps and jambons to fifteens and Paris buns. 'Hopefully Paul Hollywood and Mary Berry will come back,' says Carmel. 'We might even persuade Paul to drop one L from his surname to fit in.

'It'll be great for innuendo. Plenty of banter about cream fingers and firm baps – I can't wait to hear Paul complaining about someone's soggy fadge, or Mary giving off about a contestant's deformed gravy ring.'

The producers have already carried out auditions for the show and are said to be delighted with the results, particularly the showstopper round.

'There was a triple decker crisp sandwich – alternating layers of Nutty Crust and Spicy Bikers,' says Carmel, 'and an inside-out pastie bap – a pastie carefully cut in half, with a slice of Veda inserted in the middle.'

However the clear winner was a gigantic Rice Krispie bun – six boxes of cereal mixed with molten chocolate and poured into a huge bun-paper made out of an old *Belfast Telegraph*. 'Best use for the *Tele* I've seen in years,' Carmel explains, 'beats reading it anyway.'

We contacted Channel 4 to see if any of this was true and they chewed our bake off.

> ❝ I can't wait to hear Paul complaining about someone's soggy fadge, or Mary giving off about a contestant's deformed gravy ring. ❞

Weatherman Mitchell develops laser eyes superpower

Bosses at BBC Northern Ireland are said to be 'quaking in their boots' after their counterparts at UTV revealed that weatherman Frank Mitchell has unexpectedly acquired the laser eyes superpower.

Experts believe that Mitchell, 67, developed the condition as a result of hundreds of bouts of laser eye surgery, a process that he advertises continually through social and mainstream media along with his colleague Pamela Ballantine. 'Frank and Pamela are never off the operating table,' said a UTV insider. 'It started off as a simple matter of correcting their vision, but soon they both became addicted. After his 124th operation, Frank accidentally set fire to Paul Clarke's arse during rehearsals for *UTV Live* and so discovered that he could blast red-hot laser beams from his eyes. Pamela's had an altogether different reaction to the surgery – she's grown to over fifty feet high.'

Over at the BBC there are concerns that the newly enhanced UTV weather team will use their powers for evil, and attempt to wrest control of the small screen from their traditional rivals Barra Best and Cecilia Daly.

'We're taking steps to address this,' we were told by BBC Head of Genetic Modification Professor Charles Xavier. 'At this very moment Barra is being repeatedly bitten by radioactive spiders, in the vague hope that he'll be able to stick to walls and fire web stuff from his wrists. We're not sure what to do with Cecilia, but we've dressed her all in leather and given her a rake of cats to look after.'

'In the meantime we've sprayed Nolan green and have him wandering around Ormeau Avenue in a pair of ripped shorts,' he concluded. 'Hopefully that'll fool the UTV super villains, but really it's a normal day for Stephen.'

Bosses at BBCNI are quaking in their boots.

Oscar Pistorius' house arrest to be at flat in Rathcoole

Following his controversial release from prison, The Ulster Fry has learned that 'blade runner' Oscar Pistorius has been ordered to relocate to a flat in the North Belfast housing estate of Rathcoole to serve the remainder of his sentence at home.

Whilst the world is horrified at his release and a public campaign to reverse the decision is planned, Pistorius' laywers are surprisingly also in full agreement with public opinion and are now considering registering a late 'guilty' plea so the South African can return to prison instead.

However, local estate agent John Century, 21, has claimed the runner will enjoy a 'great life' in the area. 'He'll get full whack DLA with the state he's in. A few of my da's mates get it and they are basically legless all the time too! He'll be in his element.'

The palatial one-bedroom flat on the twelfth floor of one of Rathcoole's towering housing blocks is being renovated as we speak. 'Aye, we're installing a glass panel in the toilet door so ye can easily see who's on the bog,' revealed Century. 'Just to avoid him having any more embarrassing wee accidents outside the loo.'

The former Paralympic champion will be allowed out, but only under strict supervision.

'He's applied for a membership at the Valley Leisure Centre to start training again,' revealed area spokesman Glen Gormley. 'He also loves the fact that the Door Store is only around the corner in the Abbey Centre. He's asked them to shoot him through a couple of prices.'

Meanwhile local UVF commanders are understood to be up in arms at their new neighbour's lack of legs. 'We're talking bout a fella who shat der gurlfriend for nathing! Like nat even bout drugs or anything reasonable. If this goes tits up, how are we supposed til kneecap him?'

ULSTER'S EIGHT RUDEST PLACE NAMES

The Province of Ulster, the North of Ireland, Northern Ireland plus the Occupied Three Counties, the Occupied Six Counties plus the Free Three, the Top Bit of the Map. Whatever you want to call this bit of land we live on it has its fair share of rude place names, and being big childer at The Ulster Fry we decided to collect a few of them up.

Here's our top 8, they're mostly about willies and bums to be fair, and there'll be no prizes for guessing number 1.

1. MUFF, CO. DONEGAL
There could only ever be one number one. The village of Muff has been causing hilarity for generations. Its annual Muff Festival boasts a Miss Muff, a Little Miss Muff and even a Mayor of Muff, and the local diving club is famous around the globe. Oddly, the Co.  Derry/Londonderry village of Eglinton was also once called Muff, so double Muff action in the space of a few miles.

3. BALIX, CO. TYRONE
Not content with naming a townland Stranagalwilly, the natives of this part of Tyrone also decided to have Balix Lower and Balix  Upper just around the corner. A pair of Balixes, with a Balix Hill to go with them.

5. THE GIANT'S RING, CO. ANTRIM
Have you ever been up the Giant's Ring? It's a magnificent prehistoric site, but the archaeologists that named it should have thought of something that caused less sniggering at The Ulster Fry offices.

7. TRAILCOCK ROAD, CARRICKFERGUS, CO. ANTRIM
 Must be a quare size, if he has to trail it about after him. There's also a Trailcock Close…

2. STRANAGALWILLY, CO. TYRONE
Situated between Plumbridge and Donemanagh lies the picturesque townland of Stranagalwilly. It's more amusing if you say it quickly while drunk.

4. SEMICOCK ROAD, BALLYMONEY, CO. ANTRIM
A double whammy of rudeness here – who thought this was a good idea? And having decided it was a good idea to have Semicock Road, could they not have left it at that instead of adding Semicock  Park and Avenue? It would be nice to have a wee semi on Semicock Avenue, but most of the houses are detached.

6. CRAIGADICK, NEAR MAGHERA, CO. DERRY/LONDONDERRY
Guaranteed to liven up the long drive from Belfast to Derry, and to make matters worse it's home  to Craigadick Park and Ride. You can even stop at the picnic area and get your photo tuck. A must see tourist destination, especially if your name is Craig.

8. RINGSEND, CO. DERRY/LONDONDERRY
 It has ring in it. So it's worth a quick snigger if you're up Portrush direction.

The Predator to enter ITV's Celebrity Jungle

The ratings of *I'm a Celebrity Get Me Out of Here* are set to soar this week after ITV announced that jungle-loving alien hunter the Predator will be a contestant on the show.

'Watching people eat dingo dingleberries, racoon ringpieces and tarantula testicles was great craic for a while,' explained ITV chief Dick Whacker, 'but folk are sick to the back teeth with it now, so we're adding an extra survival element by having an invisible psychopathic alien picking off contestants with a laser cannon.'

Ant and Dec broke the news this morning, revealing that the Predator was taking the place of Lady Colin Campbell. Rather than the expected outbreak of panic, most contestants were delighted to get a better-looking replacement for the apparently famous socialite, whilst others admitted that an actual celebrity entering the show was 'wile exciting'.

However today's team challenge has not gone well after the Predator suggested that rather than compete for rations, the red team should simply eat the yellow team, kindly offering to rip out their spines and hang their carcasses from the trees.

Several technical problems have also arisen which are preventing Arnie's former nemesis from sighting his targets. 'Aye, I can't see yer doll Susannah from thon clothes show cos she's a cold-blooded bitch,' explained Mr Predator. 'Whilst some of the boring bastards are fading into the background that much they are pure camouflaged. The crafty hoors!'

The Predator is just the first in a raft of sci-fi stars set to appear on reality shows. Alan Sugar has revealed that the Alien is set to compete to be his apprentice, whilst an upcoming episode of *Catfish* shows Robocop trying to bag a date with the Terminator by letting on to be Sarah Connor.

Meanwhile the BBC are in talks with Hannibal Lecter about a role in *Celebrity Masterchef*. His suggestion of cooking the presenters in the live final has proved popular with focus groups.

> Inspired by the idea, the BBC are in talks with Hannibal Lecter about a role in *Celebrity Masterchef*.

Brangelina to split in squabble over Portrush caravan

With the world reeling from the news that celebrity power couple Angelina Jolie and Brad Pitt are sensationally set to split, The Ulster Fry can reveal some exclusive details about their dramatic parting of ways.

'They were always fighting over everything,' revealed Brad's close friend and confidant Hugo Duncan. 'He wanted beans on his fry, but Angelina thought it was rotten and turned her nose up every breakfast. Then she'd want to take the 4a bus in from Dundonald into work … but he thought the 19 was faster.

'The last straw was when Brad went ahead and watched two episodes of *Lesser Spotted Ulster* after she fell asleep last week,' he added. 'She lost the bap with him. F**ked him outta the house.'

However the couple's next-door neighbour Pamela Ballantine told us that the location of the couple's caravan was the major deciding factor in the split. 'Brad loves heading to Portrush every year, but Angie visited mine in Cranfield last summer and fancied a wee change. He was having none of it.

'The lousy bastard!' she added.

Divorce lawyers have now been brought in to divide their sizeable estate. Pitt is 'not for parting' with the 2005 Renault Espace people carrier he bought at the Mid-Ulster Auctions last year, whilst Jolie is set to fight 'tooth and nail' for the sofa they got from DFS, claiming 'he never paid f**k-all towards it and there's only three months left on the payments.'

Other family heirlooms are also on the table. 'Brad wants to hold on to the collection of pint glasses he's nicked from the Errigle down the years,' says his long-standing pal, Keith Burnside, 'but Angelina fancies them for her new flat in Rathcoole. It's gonna be a whole handlin'!'

There is no evidence that UTV weather villain Frank Mitchell was responsible for the couple's breakup, but he probably was.

Women 'just making up colour names', reveals report

A report published today by the Craigavon College of Inferior Design has shattered the long-held belief that women instinctively know shitloads of colour names that men have never even heard of.

Laughing about it today, local housewife Jane Dulux told her husband, 'Ah I was only messing with you, honey. I just thought "duck egg" sounded cooler than light green. And who wants to paint their hallway cream when it can be "bone china" or "alabaster"? I don't even know what the f**k that means, but it sounds wonderful. Are you annoyed with me now? Your wee face is turning like a Moroccan terracotta sorta colour.'

Women have long given the impression that they are born with a vast genetically enhanced vocabulary of pigmentation descriptions. However Professor Ron Seal today shed some light on this age-old belief. 'Nah, they're just talking out their hole,' he explained. 'Like seriously. Teal? Magenta? Turquoise? Lavender? Periwinkle? Load of shite. As any man will tell you, all colours in the spectrum can be easily described by mixing them together verbally.'

'Bluey-greeny, browny-yellowish or pinky-purpley. It's not rocket science, like. No one knows what f**king colour chartreuse is. But yellowy-greenish – now you're chattin.'

However campaigners at the Women's Institute for Pernicketyness have already released an updated colour swatch with complimentary 'male alternative' colour names. 'Soon men will be able to paint stuff Ferrari Red, Buckfast Purple, Chelsea Blue and Soda Farl Cream,' revealed Anne Wickes. 'We've even got ranges named after superheroes, FHM lingerie shoots and sports stars. My husband thinks it's brilliant. When I left this morning he was hitting the woodwork with a tin of Wayne Marooney.'

Yer man off *Grand Designs* campaigns to save Larne crown

Kevin Thingy off Channel 4's *Grand Designs* has joined a host of other celebrities to lead a campaign to save the iconic crown that stands in the middle of Larne's Circular Road roundabout.

'It's an amazing piece of architecture,' said the presenter, 'and one which stands proudly at the gateway to Larne, a gateway which is, in a very real sense, like a gateway to Larne.'

'What one notices first,' he went on, 'is how easily it blends into the landscape around us, its circular base mirroring the circularity of the roundabout, which in turn reflects the name of the road itself, which is Circular. And yet it rises proudly towards the heavens, resplendent against a slate grey Antrim sky. Perhaps it is telling us something about something, I would imagine.' He then said 'integrity' about six times before gazing off into the distance.

Other celebrities have thrown their architectural weight behind the campaign. That wee George Clarke fella off his *Amazing Spaces* claimed that the crown was a fine example of a thing that someone made. 'It's one of the best smallish things I've seen,' he told The Ulster Fry. 'Me and my beardy hipster friends are going to build one in the woods using only some sticks and this piece of string. Then we'll drink craft beer and talk about sheds.'

Phil Spencer off *Location, Location, Location* also loves the ginormous crown, telling us that he thought it was 'f**king class'. 'It's f**king class,' he said, 'and no doubt adds a lot to the house prices in the area. In many ways it's like the Eiffel Tower of the greater Larne area, or should that be the Eiffel Tower is like the Circular Road Crown of Paris.'

However Mid and East Antrim Council are still coming under pressure to remove the monument, with some people feeling that it is sectarian in some weird way, while others think it is a bit shit.

'We're looking at some replacement structures,' said council arts officer, Stella Sealink-Ferry, 'structures that would reflect both the bustling metropolis that is Larne and the vibrant future of Northern Ireland.'

These are believed to include an upturned bottle of Buckfast, a half-sunk Titanic and a scale model of Stephen Nolan.

> ❛ It no doubt adds a lot to house prices in the area, ❜ says Phil Spencer.

The Ulster Fry

Solution to extremism is more extremism, say so-called experts on social media

As the world struggles to come to terms with the horrific events in Paris last night, politicians, the press, celebrities and the dogs in the street have raced to social media to find someone to blame.

The geopolitical experts at the *News Letter* were quick off the mark with an editorial posted at midnight that demanded we 'hunt down and kill' Islamic extremists – a headline that even the editor of that paper felt necessary to change in the morning. Even if such a demand for action had any merit, the piece went on to insist that 'the civil liberty fools who question the work of our intelligence services must be ignored'.

A recent study into liberty and freedom showed that both are actually best achieved by their removal. The study – probably sponsored by Fox News – went on to show that allowing government agencies carte blanche to read the emails of private citizens is the perfect way to fight a terrorist group that promotes totalitarianism.

Meanwhile, former *X Factor* winner Sam Bailey, a noted expert on international affairs, was moved to tweet, 'OMG I think it's time to shut our borders.' A furious reaction from her followers led to the hurried deletion of the tweet, but not before she told her detractors to, 'pipe the fuck down'.

Elsewhere Jim Allister's TUV compared French football fans singing their national anthem on the Paris Metro last night to the Remembrance Day circus they initiated on Wednesday, and Britain First used the tragedy to encourage social media users to follow and contribute to their cause.

At the Ulster Fry we don't claim to be experts on global affairs or international terrorism, but growing up here we do know that ignorance, hate and narrow-mindedness are great attributes to have for two activities. 1) Making racist, uneducated comments on social media. 2) Being recruited by terrorists.

Anyone spreading fear and hatred through their own ignorance shouldn't let tragic irony or blatant hypocrisy get in the way of a good rant. For the rest of us, there are better places to learn about the world than Facebook and Twitter feeds.

> There are better places to learn than social media feeds.

THE ULSTER FRY COURT REPORTS

Northern Ireland is home to some of the hardest, most notorious criminals in the world. The following crimes may cause distress to some readers (especially those from Hillsborough):

62-year-old retired housewife Enya Way appeared in court after police were called to her local supermarket amid scenes of customer violence. Whilst not personally involved in the attacks, CCTV footage showed Mrs Way repeatedly stopping to casually browse shelves at the exact moment someone behind her actually needed something. Eventually other customers 'lost their shit' and starting battering each other with French baguettes and rolls of Bacofoil. 'People like you are dangerous and make me sick,' judge Gildan McTavish told her, sentencing her to six months of midnight shopping at a 24-hour Tesco.

There was drama at Newry courthouse this morning as 27-year-old local busker, Terry Stringer, appeared before a jury charged with multiple counts of murder. Several ear-witnesses recounted how Mr Stringer had brutally killed several innocent songs in broad daylight this weekend, including Radiohead's 'High and Dry', 'Firework' by Katie Perry and 'one of those annoying f**king songs by The Script'. He was found unanimously guilty and sentenced to three consecutive life sentences of winding his neck in.

47-year-old cabbie, Bonsai Adams, appeared before Belfast magistrates today charged with a litany of vicious heat crimes at his Glengormley home. His wife Flora told the court that his distressing habit of leaving the front door open was 'costing her a clean fortune' and driving her 'buck mad'. The taxi man pleaded guilty on seventy-plus charges of 'letting all the heat out' plus forty lesser charges of 'letting a wile draft in'. He was sentenced to two weeks' community service of pouring the contents of emergency home heating oil drums into people's oil tanks whilst balancing precariously on a wheelie bin.

Finally, there were emotional scenes at Derry courthouse earlier as 38-year-old driver, Cautious McCafferty, stood trial for seventeen counts of stopping at empty roundabouts to triple-check that there definitely wasn't anyone coming. Using a diagram to explain, prosecution barrister, Exhibit A Doherty, showed how Star Trek teleportation technology was only possible in movies, and that inanimate objects such as cars couldn't simply materialise in the middle of a deserted road. She was found unanimously guilty and given two consecutive life sentences following a learner driver.

Time-travelling journalists take over at *Belfast Telegraph*

In a move seemingly designed to offend many of its readers, the *Belfast Telegraph* wound back the clock today with a front-page headline that screamed '6 out of 10 babies born out of wedlock'.

The article went on to tell us that the figure referred to babies born in Belfast and Derry and that the average for Northern Ireland was in fact 4 in 10, but according to our source close to the *Belfast Telegraph* 'that wouldn't have made such a good headline'.

'As the biggest-selling paper in Northern Ireland, it's important to over-sensationalise and try and stir up as much controversy as possible,' our source told us. 'That's why the word wedlock was chosen, I mean you can't get more 1950s than that, and it's bound to get the Free Ps excited.'

As if to confirm this, the article interviewed the Revd David McIlveen, a well-known representative of one of the smallest of Northern Ireland's Christian denominations. He declared the news 'a tragedy' before stating that 'morals have been devalued, and people don't respect traditional values'. Sadly the article didn't clarify whether this would prevent the Revd McIlveen from continuing to try to force those people to follow such values.

The attention-grabbing, puritanical headline is believed to be the first in a series of retro-articles planned by *Belfast Telegraph* chiefs, who have a new recruitment policy of hiring journalists from ye olden days. The paper is offering special inducements to attract long dead scribes from beyond the grave

– pay rates have gone up to three shillings and sixpence a week, and the editor has even introduced a 'penny-farthing to work' scheme.

'We have a wonderful new reporter from Victorian times called Barnaby Chuzzlewit working on all our top stories,' we were told. 'He's covering the scandalous sale of intoxicating liquor to women, as well as the astonishing new trend for off-the-shoulder dresses.'

Meanwhile, seventeenth-century crime reporter the Revd Nathaniel Barebones is understood to be investigating some acts of vandalism on Islandmagee. 'He's like a bloodhound when it comes to crime stories,' says our source. 'Most folk think it's the local teenagers, but Revd Barebones has all the evidence he needs to prove that it's down to witches.'

THE ULSTER FRY GUIDE TO A DRUNKEN NIGHT OUT

IT'S FRIDAY AT LAST. YOU MIGHT BE PLANNING A NIGHT OUT. HERE'S OUR PREDICTION OF WHAT WILL HAPPEN …

1 GETTING READY

This used to be easy for men and complicated for women, but modern 'grooming habits' changed that. Women get together, put on 'mekup' and talk about woman stuff; men now have to apply beard oils as well as wash themselves. Unless you're a culchie, then just change shitty boots for clean boots, maybe with a checked shirt. That's for both men and women.

2 THE CARRY-OUT

In England it's 'pre-loading', in Northern Ireland it's a bottle of wine and four cans. It's also the best part of the evening. Shite can be talked without shouting and everyone is still capable of walking. It's all downhill from here.

3 THE PUB

Usually a crowded place with overpriced drinks that make you glad you had that carry-out. You queue for ages to get served because some bastard in front of you is ordering cocktails, so get double rounds in. Inevitably someone suggests shots, leading to …

4 SLABBERING

You are the font of all knowledge. Your expertise is boundless. You impress folk you fancy with witty stories and devastating put downs. You are slabbering. You will keep slabbering for the rest of the night, but right now you are the slabber-meister.

5 BAD DANCING

You may be in a bar with a dance floor, or you may go to a 'club'. You promise yourself you won't dance but eventually you yield and 'throw some shapes'. Chances are you end up …

6 FALLING ON YOUR HOLE

This can happen at any stage of the evening but usually when you step outside into fresh air and are suddenly hit by the huge quantity of alcohol you've consumed. You find a tempting piece of street furniture and attempt to vault it like an Olympic hurdler. Then you fall on your hole.

7 GRAVY CHIP

Or whatever shite your limited powers of speech allow you to order in some hole you'd avoid during the week. It's raining and you can't get a cab, so this'll sustain you on the way home. Once there you intend to finish your carry-out and keep slabbering, but stage 8 is more likely.

8 BOKING YOUR RING

There must've been something wrong with that gravy chip. Your insides are torn out as you kneel over the toilet bowl, hoping that the previous user flushed. However even as you yack your hoop into the porcelain pool, you congratulate yourself on what a great night out you've had.

9 THE MORNING AFTER

The bowel-wrenching discomfort you are suffering is nothing compared to the half-remembered snippets of slabbering that occasionally return to your mind. You check your phone for status updates, hurriedly delete the lovingly dedicated tunes you posted at 4 a.m. Then you remember you can't delete texts.

10 SUKIE AND A SAUSAGE ROLL

There can only be one cure for this sickness. You need the cool, life-giving properties of Sukie, and the stomach lining powers of a sausage roll. Crisps are also advisable as they contain vitamins and minerals essential in returning you to normality, so that you can move onto number 11 …

11 GETTING READY

Ach, sure, it's still the weekend. You may as well …

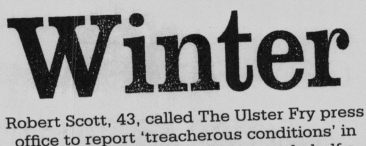

Winter

Robert Scott, 43, called The Ulster Fry press office to report 'treacherous conditions' in his native South Belfast. 'It's nearly half a centimetre deep in places,' he told us. 'I've almost fallen on my hole twice.'

Rioting mars Black Friday sales in Newtownards

Ards Shopping Centre is ablaze this evening after arguments linked to the Black Friday sales spilled over into violence.

After rioting flared this morning the PSNI was soon forced to admit that its officers had lost control of the situation and that mob rule was in force. A spokesman advised shoppers either to avoid the area completely, or to bring their own weapons.

Comber shopper Thomas Cook admits walking over fellow shoppers to get the last remaining Millenium Falcon for his son. 'Our Willie's already got one of these but this will do as a spare,' he beamed. 'It was down from £39.99 to £39.49 – you couldn't resist a bargain like that.'

His friend Bob Marche told us that he'd been sleeping in the car park since Tuesday, just so that he could be one of the first people into Poundland. 'It was all worth it,' he boasted, 'although I almost didn't get this pack of forty-eight AA batteries. I had to wrestle some auld doll in a wheelchair who put her hand on them first. Seeing as how it's Black Friday, I thought I'd get into the spirit by kicking her shins and then tipping her out of the wheelchair on to the floor.'

We also understand that one woman from the Scrabo Estate broke eight ribs in a crush at the doors of Primark but still managed to get her hands on a pair of pyjamas reduced from £8 to £6. 'I had to fracture a few skulls with my walking stick,' she revealed, 'but I got these Betty Boop jammies and a Superman onesie for our Cecil.'

Elsewhere two pregnant teens were seen ramming each other with prams outside Claire's Accessories. 17-year-old Sue Zone explained, 'I waited all morning to get our Beyoncé a half-price tiara and then this tramp tried to jump the queue.'

Speaking from his bed in the Ulster Hospital, a spokesman for the shopping centre has declared the Black Friday sales 'a great success'.

> 'I thought I'd get into the spirit by kicking her shins.'

Next episode of *The Fall* set entirely in queue at Boojum

Writers of hit Belfast TV show *The Fall* have upped the gritty realism of the locally set psychological thriller by confirming that serial killer Paul Spector, played by Jamie Dornan, will spend an entire episode of the show waiting patiently in a ridiculously long queue for a burrito.

The BBC, which has come under criticism of late for portraying Belfast as an unnecessarily sinister and dark place, today released details of the episode, confirming that Ulster's favourite dreamboat psychopath will take a much-needed break from brutally killing women to queue alongside a collection of other bearded men before viciously attacking a burrito.

Writers confirmed that Spector will also spot his next victim in the popular themed restaurant but will be unable to follow her as he'll be too anxious about losing his place in the line of burrito addicts.

'We wanted to give fans around the world a real taste of Belfast,' said the show's principal scriptwriter Tangent O'Neill, 'which, as everyone knows, is Mexican.'

'Spector has returned to the city against his better judgement. He's back at work, back preying on women and trying to put his family back together. All whilst the police close in on him. These are tough, challenging times. However, to further compound his frustration, he only gets a forty-five-minute lunch break, so we

wanted to explore the tension of this predicament with our viewers.'

Audiences are expected to be on the edges of their seats during the gripping queue-based episode, as the strain of getting served, eating a burrito the size of a used nappy and getting back to his desk on time builds to a climax.

'Aye. He's got an important two o'clock appointment,' confirmed O'Neill.

The first two seasons of the show prompted women across the Province to experience a huge wave of mixed emotions, as they hid behind/humped pillows in fear/delight, whilst watching evil/gorgeous psychopath/hunk Jamie Dornan brutally murder/feel-up a string of unlucky/lucky women.

Riots rock Holywood as sports personality anger grows

Rioting has broken out in North Down this morning as anger about the results of last night's *BBC Sports Personality of the Year* result tipped over into violence.

The trouble flared after racing driver Lewis Hamilton pipped local boy Rory McIlroy to the coveted *SPOTY* title, with the news bringing hundreds of angry golf fans onto the streets of Holywood to protest at the perceived injustice.

Protesters have daubed pro-McIlroy graffiti on several public buildings and a mural declaring 'You are now entering Free Holywood – please drive carefully' has been painted on to a gable end on Church Road.

Cars produced by Hamilton's team Mercedes were hijacked and set on fire in the High Street

area and it is believed that the committee of Holywood Golf Club has established an army council to co-ordinate military action. The army has defused an improvised explosive device attached to an abandoned golf buggy outside a local Mercedes dealership, and we understand that Hamilton has received threatening parcels containing live golf balls.

Local resident Albert Sphincter

is acting as a spokesman for the rioters. 'All Hamilton does is drive round in circles,' he claimed, 'whereas our boy drives all over the fairway.'

We tried to contact Rory McIlroy for comment, but were told by his agent that he is 'presently indisposed' as he is helping police with their enquiries following an incident involving Gary Lineker's arse and a 5-iron.

Ninety five per cent of Belfast men under thirty 'now have beards', say police

Police in Belfast are becoming concerned that they will soon be unable to identify criminals, due to the increasingly high number of beards sported by young men in the city.

According to a study conducted for the PSNI by Larne School of Economics 'most under 30s are expressing their individuality by looking exactly the same, opting to ponce about the city centre like pasty-faced polar explorers.'

The report claims that this is making the successful identification of criminals virtually impossible – a situation made worse by other similarities. 'Almost all are wearing tweed jackets that are slightly too small and around fifty per cent have one arm heavily tattooed with tribal images that bear

no relationship to the cultural background of the individual.'

A PSNI spokesman has confirmed that there is a growing beard-related problem, but said that the police had the situation under control. 'The rise in beard wearing has been matched by a fall in the crime rate,' he explained. 'Most young men are too busy comparing and combing their facial hair to commit any crimes, with few prepared to risk their beards in a violent confrontation.'

'Bunch of dicks,' he added.

Harland & Wolff to build new Death Star

Following The Ulster Fry's recent exclusive that Darth Vader had been appointed head of the DUP, we've learned that work has already started on a new Death Star at Belfast shipyard, Harland & Wolff.

Lord Vader wants to revitalise Northern Ireland's ailing shipbuilding industry and has started by awarding a defence contract believed to be worth 250 trillion space credits. Aside from boosting the local economy, the deal will also generate thousands of new jobs for local people, especially those eager to wear gigantic plastic helmets at work.

Disney spokesman Mickey Duck told us, 'The last two Death Stars were spectacularly destroyed shortly after being built. With a legacy like that to uphold we didn't want to take a chance using any old shipyard. Not only can Northern Ireland build ships that epically fail on their maiden voyage – but yes can make a mountain of cash off it for decades afterwards!'

'Anyone who has bought any second-hand shite from George Lucas recently will respect this sort of track record,' he added.

Work is already underway at Belfast Harbour and the port was bustling today with hundreds of weird-looking creatures that talk funny. 'Aye, due to demand we've been forced to employ people from as far away as Ballymena,' explained a spokesman. 'No one really knows what the f**k they are saying like … even C-3PO was all like "Ye wha?" But they seem well on board with the whole Star Wars theme. A few have already gone with their sisters.'

Lord Vader arrived on site today to motivate the workforce with his often-say-die attitude to failure, but we missed our chance to speak to him in person. 'I'm afraid it's to late for you, big son,' his aide told us. 'He's gone over to the port side.'

> **Work is already underway at Belfast Harbour and the port was bustling today with hundreds of weird-looking creatures that talk funny.**

Craigavon woman jailed after becoming addicted to decorative signs

A County Armagh woman has been jailed for two years after her addiction to covering her house in crap decorative signs spilled over into violence.

34-year-old Arlene Thomson, who cannot be named for legal reasons, says that the trigger for her addiction was the gift of a hilarious bathroom sign which declared, 'If you sprinkle when you tinkle, please be neat and wipe the seat.'

'Pretty soon she was hanging these things all over the house,' says her husband Barry. 'We had signs in the kitchen saying "I love cooking with wine, sometimes I even put it in the food" and "Mum's cafe". Everything had labels on it.

In the bathroom she had carved wooden letters spelling out stuff like "BATH", "SHOWER" and "TOWELS" as if we're all too stupid to know what the things are. Why do I need a sign that says "HOME" on it? I know when I'm home.

'The worst ones were the lifestyle ones,' claims Barry. 'She had loads of plaques and pictures saying stuff like "Love is at the heart of this home", "Life is Beautiful" and "Sun, Sand, Ocean". We live in Craigavon, FFS.'

According to her solicitor, Mrs Thomson's addiction worsened after the 'Keep calm and carry on' craze. 'Arlene became completely incapable of remaining calm unless she had a sign which instructed her to do so,' stated Albert Check, of Lurgan solicitors Cash, Orr, Check.

'For example, she was okay making tea if she'd seen the "Keep calm and put the kettle on" sign, but flew into a rage when doing her grocery shopping because she hadn't seen "Keep calm and go down to the butchers for half a pound of sausages". As a result Mrs Thomson assaulted four shopkeepers over a three-week period.'

Passing sentence, District Judge Edward Dread said it was one of the worst cases of sign addiction he'd ever seen.

No one from TK Maxx was available for comment.

New PSNI unit to target 'boy racers'

The PSNI has released details of a new traffic branch unit that will specifically target young males driving so-called 'hot hatches'.

'The Boy Racer Division is currently undergoing special training tailored to allow them to first recognise, and then eradicate these roadside menaces,' said Superintendent Brian Cant.

This training focuses on identifying the racers at an early stage. 'The first indicator of "boy racer" status is the type of motor that they drive,' explains Cant. 'Generally it's a fairly decrepit hatchback worth about 50 quid – typically a Fiesta or a 106 – that has been sprayed bright orange, lowered to about an inch off the ground and then laden with immense speakers that wouldn't be out of place at

the Glastonbury Festival. It isn't unusual for the owners to spend upwards of £3000 on modifying these vehicles, turning them from MOT-scraping rust buckets into uninsurable death traps.'

The second part of the process is recognising the traits of the drivers themselves. 'Whilst out of their vehicles they can be spotted by their unusual dress sense – I mean who really wants to wear a jacket covered in adverts for oil companies and Scania lorries?' says unit trainee Constable Floella Benjamin. 'When they're driving they're even easier to spot, as their seats are so far back they can barely reach the pedals, and so low that they must be using their arses to brake.'

Once operational the new unit will focus on known boy racer locations. 'They meet in car parks, park in a line and talk shite about girls and diesel, before attempting a doughnut and then going home to their mums,' says Superintendent Cant. 'We'll lift them there, or catch them when they're counting loose change so they can stick £5 worth of fuel in their motor.'

A spokesboy for the Northern Ireland Association of Doughnutters, 21-year-old Dungiven teenager Johnny Ball, reacted angrily to the news.

'We put literally millions of pounds into the public purse every year, mostly in fines to be honest, but some of us even pay our road tax as well,' he claimed indignantly, before speeding off to do handbrake turns on the Glenshane Pass.

Belfast to bring in overtaking lanes on pavements

The move comes amid growing concerns about pavement rage incidents.

Following the introduction of a new 20 mph speed limit and bus lane cameras in the city centre, councillors in Belfast have finally bowed to pressure from fast-walking pedestrians to introduce a lane system on the city's footpaths.

The move comes amid growing concerns about a spate of 'pavement rage' incidents that have seen speedier pedestrians getting stuck behind slow-moving shoppers. There have also been reports of walkers being forced to use the bus lane to overtake conversational pensioners entirely blocking the footpaths.

'There'll be a four-lane, two-way system on the wider pavements – a slow lane and an overtaking lane in each direction,' says council spokesman Sean Dander. 'On narrower stretches we'll be constructing lay-bys so folk can pull in and allow others to pass.'

The new system will be policed by 'fast lane' cameras to ensure that pedestrians don't cause unnecessary hold-ups, with stiff fines for those who do. The council will use facial software at first, though they are plans to require pavement users to wear front and rear number plates in the city centre.

However, according to the council, the move isn't designed to raise revenue, but is driven by fears for pedestrian safety. 'The two-way system is essential. No one wants to see a repeat of November's twelve-person pile-up that took place outside the Europa,' says Dander.

Despite this there will still be a boost for the local economy. 'People being late for work because they get stuck behind lumbering lard-arses in the morning costs us nearly £12 million in lost productivity each year,' explains council accountant Walter House-Cooper. 'We can also use the money raised by fines to reinvest in the pavement network, as well as spending it on trips for councillors to look at sidewalks in Florida.'

A similar plan for supermarket aisles has been shelved.

Downton Abbey relocates to Newtownabbey in dazzling Christmas plot twist

As viewers eagerly await the Christmas episode of the popular boring TV show *Downton Abbey*, The Ulster Fry can exclusively reveal that the producers have torn up the costume drama rulebook by relocating the cast to Rathcoole.

In the stunning departure, the Earl of Grantham has fallen on hard times and has moved his extended family to south Antrim. Despite his fall from grace, the Earl's breeding and air of superiority have ensured that he has risen to the very top in his new social circle.

'I play "Mad Rab" Crawley,' says cast member Hugh Bonneville, 'a local UDA brigadier with a penchant for flowery shirts, fast cars and Tennent's Super. The accent's been a bit of a struggle, I admit. It took a while to get from "yes Mama" to "aye yer ma" but I don't think your local viewers will notice.'

Not all of the Earl's family have found the transition to Rathcoole life so easy. The Dowager Countess, played by Maggie Smith, is understood to be struggling to survive on her meagre pension, and is seen eagerly awaiting her Winter Fuel Payment.

'Lady Violet is having a hard time,' says Smith. 'The electricity board have arrived and installed a new meter so now the magnets won't work. The Earl would have her put in a home if there were any still left open.'

Meanwhile Mad Rab's faithful servant, the war veteran Mr Bates, has lost his DLA payments and has been forced to take on a car wash job at a disused petrol station near the Abbey Centre. 'It's not exactly the valeting he's used to,' says Bonneville, 'but I suppose it's a step up from wiping the hole of an aristocrat.'

The show's change in direction has met with a mixed response from the critics. Some have hailed it as a radical shift towards genuine social commentary; others feel it has betrayed a much-loved formula. However everyone agrees that even if it's completely shite, it'll be better than the *Mrs Brown's Boys Christmas Special.*

ULSTER FRYGRANCES – NINE PERFUMES & COLOGNES FOR NORN IRON

Stuck for gift ideas for that awkward hoor in your life? Why not check out our exciting range of NI perfumes and aftershaves, specially selected for the Ulster market. There's something for everywan …

CALVIN KLEIN'S CK WAN

GUESS WHA?

HUGO DUNCAN

BIGOTRY FOR MEN

CHANNEL NO. 9
FOR THE DERRY WANS

LYNX CRAIGAVON AND LYNX STRABANE

PSNI

YEE SLABBERING LAD?

OLD SPIDE

Ten last-minute gift ideas
FOR NORN IRON

If you are anything like us you probably haven't bothered your hole to start Christmas shopping yet. To help in your hour of need (typically 4 p.m. – 5 p.m. on Christmas Eve for us) we've compiled a helpful list of some of Norn Iron's most sought-after gifts and toys.

Which take your fancy?

1. DISNEY'S FOUNDERED

2. MAY MCFETTRIDGE MAKE-UP DOLL

3. PLAYMOBIL TRANSLINK EDITION

4. THE MICRASAFT XBAX WAN

5. A LOCK OF GAMES FOR YOUR XBAX WAN

6. 'GERRY WHO?' MYSTERY BOARD GAME

7. THE EAMONN HOLMES BREAKFAST TV

8. LEGO TITANIC

9. BABY'S FIRST BONFIRE SET

10. GAME OF THRONES BUCK 'N' DIE BOARD GAME

'Old King Billy' tops Northern Ireland poetry poll

The classic playground limerick 'Old King Billy had a ten-foot willy' has been voted Northern Ireland's favourite poem in a survey conducted by the University of East Strabane.

The meaning of the rhyme – which reads:

Old King Billy had a ten-foot
willy,
so he showed it to the woman
next door,
she thought it was a snake,
and hit it with a rake,
and now it's only five foot four

– has long been a puzzle to academics.

Dr Edwin Vole, Professor of Big Words at the university, said that the poem is 'beautiful in its simplicity' but that it has 'echoes of the sectarian struggle in Northern Ireland'.

'For some, King Billy represents the dominant position of Unionism,' he explained, 'while the woman next door takes the role of the Nationalist minority.

'A struggle ensues, and the woman lashes out, striking a blow at the symbolic manhood of King Billy, leaving over four foot of his appendage on her side of the fence. Despite this, King Billy retains the majority of his member and it remains impressive in length.'

The *Guardian*'s poetry critic Esmerelda Hare thinks differently. 'It is clearly a metaphor for the battle of the sexes, with the woman next door representing the rise of the feminist movement. She manages to take away some of his power, but that core inequality still exists. We are, of course, left to wonder what she struck him with – a rake of what exactly?'

However 8-year-old Jack Hedgehog, who participated in the survey, disagreed with both academics. 'I like it because it has the word willy in it,' he said, 'and willies are funny.'

Another children's rhyme 'Milk, milk, lemonade / Round the corner chocolate's made' came second in the poll, followed by 'Ip dip dog shit'. Seamus Heaney's 'Digging' was just outside the top three.

Local man expects hero's welcome for getting to work in 'snow'

A Belfast civil servant is expecting his bosses to spend the day congratulating him after he successfully negotiated a bit of slush on the way to work this morning.

Forty-three year-old Robert Scott, who wishes to remain anonymous, called The Ulster Fry press office to report 'horrific conditions' in his native South Belfast. 'It's nearly half a centimetre deep in places,' he told us, as he braved the icy conditions. 'I've almost fallen on my hole twice, but fortunately I've been able to regain my balance thanks to the snow shoes I bought in November.'

Even so, the intrepid Mr Scott found his journey down the Lisburn Road particularly perilous.

'I'm pretty sure I saw a polar bear near Ryan's Bar,' he revealed, 'at least I saw a big white thing about the size of a car. I felt like

Leonardo DiCaprio in that film where he fights the bear, except I wasn't attacked or anything, and my bear just sat there in its parking space.'

Despite this shock the bearded explorer was able to make good speed towards the city centre. 'The huskies almost lost it in Shaftesbury Square, but I managed to get the sled back on track and down Great Victoria Street.

'It was a f**king nightmare parking them, I'll tell ye, but finally I found somewhere behind Castlecourt. They're on a double yellow, but I didn't feed them this morning and the chances are they'd eat any traffic warden that goes near them.'

Mr Scott is now at his desk regaling colleagues with stories of his daring journey, and waiting for his manager to arrive to see if the conditions are bad enough for her to send him home.

Gerrard enticed by attractive 'Sporting Lisburn' offer

Bookmakers have suspended all betting on Steven Gerrard's next club amid rumours that the Liverpool captain has already agreed terms with local side Lisburn Distillery.

The move came after Gerrard was spotted getting off the 238 Goldliner at Sprucefield before climbing into a waiting New City cab to be spirited away for talks with club officials. As yet there has been no confirmation from either club, but our unnamed source at Liverpool, right back Glen Johnson, told us that Gerrard was a longstanding admirer of the Lisburn side.

'Distillery's is always the first result that Stevie looks for after we come off the pitch,' said Johnson. 'He was always banging on about wanting to finish his career playing for "the Whites". We thought he was talking about Real Madrid, but it looks like we had the wrong "los Blancos".'

Surprisingly it turns out that the one-time England captain has a hankering for all things Northern Ireland. 'He likes nothing more than a pastie bap before a game,' Johnson told us, 'and usually has Irish music going on the team bus – a bit of Van Morrison, maybe some Philomena Begley. To be honest, it seems like the right move for him, although it'll be a big step-up in quality from what he's used to at Liverpool.'

It seems like the move would go down well with Gerrard's wife, Alex. According to her close friend and fellow WAG Coleen Rooney, 'she's well into her shopping and socialising, so she'll love the big city atmosphere in Lisburn. She'll have the Bow Street Mall on her doorstep and that big Marksies up at Sprucefield. When my Wayne and the England lads come over they can always head to the bright lights of Banbridge and hit the Coach or the Bannville for a bit of clubbing.'

Distillery manager Tommy Kincaid said he was hopeful that the move would be completed 'within days' but insisted that Gerrard would have to prove himself to his new teammates. 'Obviously he won't walk straight into the first XI. He'll need time to adapt to the pace and skill levels of Irish League football, and will be competing for his place against proven performers like Jimmy McIlhagga.'

'This could be massive boost for football here,' IFA President Jim Shaw told The Ulster Fry. 'We don't get many world-class performers, outside the big Belfast clubs anyway, and for a player of Gerrard's standard to have the opportunity to play at the likes of the Welders and Ballyclare Comrades? It's just brilliant for him. We know Liverpool don't want to sell to a competitor club, but the chances are they won't meet Distillery unless it's in a European competition. Given Liverpool's form, that seems unlikely for the foreseeable future.'

Gerrard was spotted getting off the 238 Goldliner at Sprucefield.

Medium Ormo – £3.50

Thai Sweet Chilli on Italian Granary with a splash of balsamic vinegar – £7.95

SIMPLY CRISPY
Crisp Sandwich Cafe

~~Pickled Onion Space~~ Raiders in a Belfast Bap with a Wotsit side-salad – £5.95

Daily Special Monster Munch on Ormo £3.95

No Crusts? No Problem! Add 50p

SIMPLY CRISPY
1. PICK CRISPS
2. CHOOSE BREAD
3. BUTTER OR

Crisp sandwich gets new lease of life in hip Belfast eatery

A new restaurant is aiming to give a trendy makeover to that staple of the Northern Irish dinner table – the humble crisp sandwich. Inspired by the 'Cereal Cafe' recently opened in London by two Belfast brothers, restaurateur Gavin Spleen hopes that his new venture – Simply Crispy – will attract similar success.

Situated in Belfast's fashionable Cathedral Quarter, Simply Crispy puts a new twist on a local favourite. Diners will be able choose from a menu of gourmet crisp sandwiches, or create their own delicacy from an exciting range of breads, crisps and spreads. Whether it be the staple Tayto Cheese and Onion on Sunblest sliced pan with Flora, or the more exotic Thai Sweet Chilli on Italian Granary with a splash of balsamic vinegar – the choice is almost limitless.

'Simply Crispy will cater for all tastes, and all pockets,' explained Gavin. 'Hungry carnivores will love our Beef Mini Chips on Medium Ormo, a bargain at £3.50 (crusts off 50p extra), while veggies might like to try Pickled Onion Space Raiders in a Belfast Bap with a Wotsit side-salad for a mere £5.95.

Our *piéce de resistance* is the 'Inner Ring' – a slice of Nutty Krust lovingly rolled into a thin sausage then inserted delicately through a series of Tayto Onion Rings, garnished with parsley and crushed Pringles.'

Hugo Hamilton, Restaurant Critic and Chief Hipster at Belfast style magazine *Le Ganch*, says that the city is crying out for just this kind of cafe. 'It's bound to attract the luncheon crowd, office workers eager for somewhere new and refreshing,' says Hamilton, 'and is ideal for a light bite on an evening out with friends, both bearded and otherwise. It has just the right ambience with its homespun decor of old school desks and bean bag chairs, and the food is presented so delightfully on reclaimed scaffolding boards.'

Situated in a converted public toilet on Talbot Street, as yet Simply Crispy can't serve alcohol. 'For the moment we'll be serving traditional Ulster soft drinks like Sukies, Maine's Brown Lemonade and McDaid's Football Special, but that'll change when we get the licence,' Gavin told us, 'Then we'll serve out of date Harp.'

DUP and Sinn Féin clash over TV weather maps

Stormont witnessed extraordinary scenes yesterday as a heated debate developed over the religious make-up of the towns that feature on local television weather reports.

The argument began after Sinn Féin MLA Aimsir Fliuch asked the culture minister if the department would introduce legislation to ensure that Irish language place names could be added to the BBC weather map.

According to Ms Fliuch, her constituents in West Tyrone are unable prepare for the day's weather as they were baffled by the names of foreign-sounding places like Omagh and Strabane. 'How are you supposed to know if you need a coat if you can't tell where you are?' she demanded, before tweeting her followers about the debate to prove that she actually did something the odd time.

When the minister replied that the Executive would consider the matter, there was an angry response from DUP North Antrim MLA

Gusty Day. 'My staff and I have been recording which towns have been shown on TV weather maps,' he shouted, brandishing a sheet of A4, 'and this graph proves that no less than 64 per cent of those towns are Catholic towns. Some of them are even in the Free State. Where is the parity of esteem here?'

As a result of the debate BBC NI and UTV executives have this morning agreed to choose places based on their religion on a strictly 50/50 basis in future, and to show all place names in English, Irish and Ulster-Scots.

Likewise, Frank Mitchell will ensure that his weather-watching camera includes flags and murals of different persuasions on alternate days. He has also asked viewers to let him know the religious origins of the children for whom they request birthday greetings in order to ensure they don't accidentally end up on the same segment as one of themuns.

The newly created Parity of Televisual Weather Output Commissioner, who will be paid from the education budget, will monitor the relevant programmes.

Tesco weighs into Ashers row by banning gay croissants

Tesco has sensationally joined the Ashers gay cake debate by announcing that in future it will only sell straight croissants.

The supermarket giant claims that it is bowing to customer demand, saying that homophobic shoppers are unable to cope with the traditionally bent French pastries.

'Our customers are worried that gay food items will have a negative influence on their children,' says head of product development, Geoff Shelf. 'So we're looking at

our entire range to see where we can eradicate anything with gay overtones.'

After dealing with the gay croissants, the store will be moving on to other products. 'Muller Fruit Corners are high on the list,' says Shelf, 'along with fairy cakes and Camp Coffee.

'In fact our entire fruit and veg section will be getting a revamp,' he continued. 'It'll need renamed the Heterosexual and Veg section for a start, then we'll introduce

straight bananas and Blue Lady apples. At the butcher's counter we'll no longer stock mince, but you will be able to buy a pound of manly walk.'

Gay rights campaigners are understandably furious at the news, with many calling for a boycott of the chain.

They have been joined in the action by a group of sexually active older ladies, furious that the supermarket still hasn't changed the name of tarts.

Woman accidentally summons devil in Ards Shopping Centre

A Newtownards woman is said to be 'in shock but otherwise unharmed' after she inadvertently conjured up Satan whilst shopping at her local branch of Argos.

43-year-old Agnes Toucan visited the store in search of new curling tongs, and selected set number 13 on page 666 of the Argos catalogue. Having missed the significance of the numerology when she ordered, she also failed to notice her mistake when she arrived at 'collection point A' to pick up her item, and bundled Satan into a Primark bag before loading him into the boot of her Nissan Micra.

'It wasn't until I got home that I realised my mistake,' said Agnes, 39. 'I was going out that night but when I went to style my hair it suddenly clicked. "This isn't a set of Babyliss curling tongs," I thought to myself. "This is the Prince of Darkness."

'It ruined my night out,' she explained. 'His fiery breath might work reasonably well as a hairdryer, but if anything it straightened rather than curled my hair. I must have looked a right sight.'

Fortunately Miss Toucan, 24, had retained her receipt so she was able to take the offending 'fallen angel' back to Argos where she received a full refund, and profuse apologies from store manager David Parrot. 'This kind of thing does happen occasionally,' said Mr Parrot. 'So although Satan was in full working order we were able to give her a cash refund rather than store credit. Now we're stuck with him, though, as he's been opened.'

Speaking through an interpreter, Lucifer told The Ulster Fry that while he hadn't been expecting to spawn on the Ards Peninsula, he was happy with his treatment by the staff at Argos. 'They've set me up with a job delivering stuff for them, and I've got a nice flat in Ballyhalbert,' he growled. 'I mean it could be worse. I might have been conjured from the pits of hell, only to end up in Larne.'

January to last 'another three weeks' say scientists

After years of complaints that it's 'a wile long month' scientists have discovered that January is set to continue for 'another two to three weeks'. The boffins jumped into action yesterday after reports of being 'ridiculously skint' poured in from across the country – with many people forced to borrow money to buy cheap bog roll, packets of Pasta 'n' Sauce, soup and other stuff from the weird tinned food aisle in Lidl.

January, the mysterious month that succeeds the exuberant Christmas period, has, according to historians, been known to last up to eleven weeks. During this bleak time families are often forced to quit shopping and live off variants of 'cupboard surprise' – which Wikipedia describes as 'a random meal comprised of whatever the feck you can find around the house'.

Jim Windolene, a security guard at Antrim Tesco, told us that the place had been 'deserted for weeks' and that he'd been surviving on lunch rations of loaf-heel spam sandwiches, buttered with tartare sauce. However his spirits were lifted by reports that a nearby bank machine still gave out fivers.

Experts at Larne School of Economics admitted that the situation was 'bleak' after an emergency calendar survey showed that recent skintness was set to continue until 'almost February'. This has set off local religious crackpots who have taken to street corners to predict the coming of 'Pay Day', a long-foretold prophecy that claims a powerful mysterious being will deposit money into your bank account at the end of a month.

The idea has been slammed as 'ridiculous' by leading paytheist Dickhard Rawkins though. 'The notion of some unseen entity putting funds into your bank account is as ridiculous as that of a magical Spaghetti God who watches over you,' he laughed, as he frantically searched his cupboard for some sort of sauce to go with the pasta he'd found.

January was unavailable for comment as it was too busy dragging on forever.

UTV's Frank Mitchell confesses to shameful deception

UTV weatherman Frank Mitchell spoke of his 'utter shame' today, after it was discovered that he had been making up town names for UTV's *Weather Watch* for more than five years.

Weather Watch has been a regular fixture on UTV for years, with Mitchell giving clues about the weather-watch camera's mystery location through a series of cryptic puns. However he admits he 'grew weary' of the charade, and that out of a sense of 'dangerous excitement' he began making up places whilst showing photos of Aughnacloy from different angles.

Suspicions were first raised after a local map-maker went missing trying to find towns Frank mentioned, including Magherafeltip, Ballycushenpushin, Lisnaskeaslope and Castledawsons Creek.

'I would like to apologise to UTV viewers for betraying their trust,' said Mitchell this morning. 'My actions spiralled out of control and I became addicted to the thrills of making up new towns. I just couldn't stop myself.'

The scandal doesn't end there though. The NI Census team also discovered that based on the number of children Frank has wished happy birthday to on the show, the Province is almost twelve thousand people short. It has thus further transpired that Mitchell has also been wishing 'happy birthday' to imaginary children for decades.

Dungannon man Declan Fray, now 28, revealed that a photo of himself aged 7, which his mum sent to UTV two decades ago, has been used on the channel hundreds of times under fake names. 'I've been Cormac, Benny, Jake, Larry, Barry, Logan, Eoin, Mickey, Sean, Jonny, Casper, Norman and even a Lucy thanks to a questionable mullet. I've held my silence long enough. Frank

Mitchell is a tyrant and he must be stopped.'

UTV insists Frank was acting alone in the scandal and have removed him from his job of announcing rain with immediate effect. A pale and shaken Mitchell left home this morning vowing to face his demons by checking into a private rehab facility.

'Aye, it's in Gortnabunion, away up past Ballyhalberteinstein,' he told us, before driving towards Aughnacloy.

> He began making up places whilst showing photos of Aughnacloy from different angles.

Next season of *The Walking Dead* to be set in Europa Bus Centre

After several gritty seasons scavenging for survival in the backwater slums of mid-America, hit TV show *The Walking Dead* is set to move to Northern Ireland.

Heartened by the success of *Game of Thrones*, AMC have scoured Ulster for suitably dreary locations for the apocalyptic thriller, and reportedly got 'dead excited' about the desolate bleakness of the Great Northern Mall and adjoining Translink terminals.

The Ulster Fry understands that when the show returns in the autumn, Rick and co. will initially be holed up in the nearby Spires Mall. Despite being zombie-free and totally secure, the group will be forced to seek refuge elsewhere, after everyone tells Rick that the unnecessarily loud hourly ringing of the massive church bell is doing their head in. 'It's supposed to be a f**king shopping centre,' says Daryl in a tense stand-off with the leader.

In their toughest challenge yet, the group will make their way up Great Victoria Street, where they will face an army of anti-abortion campaigners – who are aggressively looking for petitions signed – before being savagely hounded to go on a bus tour by dead-eyed monsters in bright red coats. It is understood that the group will eventually make it to the Europa side entrance when, after fighting off a horde of eager black taxi drivers, one unidentified lead cast member will be dragged into the Grand Opera House for a career-killing three-month stint in pantomime. 'It's horrific,' said a source.

Cannibalism is another recurring major theme this year too: despite the terminal having lots of food, everyone decides they would rather eat each other than an eternity of pre-packed sandwiches, flame-grilled steak McCoys crisps and bottles of Oasis in a bus station. 'I've done my time at university, Rick. I'm not going back to living like that!' shouts an impassioned Glenn, shortly before eating someone.

Filming for the season will begin shortly, with AMC reportedly 'delighted' by Translink's offer to supply free zombie extras. 'Aye, we just told them to film in the early mornings when civil servants and office workers are begrudgingly shuffling into work,' said Translink boss George '8A' Romero.

'Trust me, they won't be able to tell the difference,' he added.

SEVEN WAYS TO DRIVE YOUR MAN WILD IN BED THIS VALENTINE'S DAY

As we revealed recently, Northern Irish men are the most romantic in the world, so women across the country are now looking for ideas that will drive their men mad in the bedroom.

Juanita Twix from Belfast lifestyle magazine *Women's Problems* reveals her top tips to press all his buttons between the sheets.

1. TELL HIM YOU'VE LEFT THE IMMERSION HEATER ON.

'Men love a bit of hot stuff in the wee small hours,' says Juanita, 'so why not wait 'til 2 a.m. and tell him you think you left the immersion running. He'll be up and ready for action in seconds.'

2. BRING THE DOG TO BED.

'According to a recent survey for our magazine 74 per cent of men fantasise about having a threesome, so bringing the dog to bed should fulfil his wildest desires. Probably.'

3. REMIND HIM TO PUT THE BINS OUT.

'Give him a nudge at 4 a.m. on a Thursday morning,' says Juanita, 'and whisper in his ear "I want you to take me, right now, I want you to take me bins out."'

4. PHONE YOUR MOTHER.

'Telephone sex is a real turn on,' Juanita explains, 'so ring his bell at midnight with a forty-minute chat with your mother about who's died.'

5. EAT TOAST

'This is best done in the morning, when he's not around. Then when he slips between the sheets in the evening he'll know he's guaranteed a night of rough action. Be sure to nibble it on his side of the bed though, or what's left of his side …'

6. TAKE UP THE WHOLE BED

'Why not experiment with a few different positions?' Juanita asks. 'Try lying across the middle of the bed with pillows and cushions arranged all round your body. If you get your moves just right, you'll really push him over the edge.'

7. SUGGEST SOME DIY TASKS.

'An opportunity for more naughty talk. "Are you up for doing some dirty stuff big boy? Yeah? Great, cos the kids have blocked the ensuite toilet with baby wipes." He'll have his plunger out in no time.'

Mr Taytos to do battle on Frampton undercard

As Belfast prepared for the Carl Frampton v Chris Avalos fight, promoter Barry McGuigan announced a major addition to the event. 'We've got the Tandragee Mr Tayto up against Dublin's Mr Tayto in what is sure to be a hard-fought contest,' said the former world champion.

'The potato-weight championship of all Ireland is at stake for these two well seasoned competitors,' McGuigan told The Ulster Fry. 'In many ways it is the fight we've all been waiting for – to be honest, I'm a bit worried that it might overshadow Frampton's own bout.'

The grudge match is guaranteed to interest boxing fans as the two rivals had exchanged cross-border blows for decades before reaching an uneasy peace in recent years. 'The truce ended when down south Mr Tayto upped the ante and opened that theme park,' says McGuigan. 'Northern Ireland Mr Tayto felt fairly secure in his castle up to that point, but if

you've got a theme park? The sky's the limit.'

Each fighter will don the colours of his bestselling flavour, with the County Armagh competitor in his traditional yellow and the Dublin spud sporting his politically suspect red, white and blue cheese-and-onion branding. 'The crowd will love it,' claims McGuigan. 'Most of them will be blocked so watching two giant potatoes punching each other will make perfect sense.'

The winner of the bout will pick up a multi-pack purse containing bags weighing substantially less than individual packets, before going on to fight Gary Lineker for the world title.

> The winner of the bout will pick up a multi-pack purse weighing substantially less than individual packets.

Seventy four per cent of NI women think they'd knock Carl Frampton's ballix in, reveals report

Ahead of his much anticipated title unification fight with Scott Quigg tonight, a survey carried out on the streets of Belfast revealed that almost three quarters local women think they'd be able to give Carl Frampton 'a good hiding'.

'Sure he's only a wee squirt,' laughed Amanda Box on Royal Avenue today. 'My ex was twice the size of him and I could knock him out with a single jab – but that's one of the perks of being a pharmacist.'

Fellow shopper Sandra Millis agreed. 'I reckon I'd batter him,' she said. 'He hasn't got much hair to pull admittedly, but sure ye'd just get him in a headlock, sit on him and then give him stingy nipple twisters until he gave up. It would be wee buns.'

Her friend Abbey Newtown agreed. 'He might be okay at taking digs from boys wearing them big padded gloves,' she said, 'but any self-respecting Belfast girl with a full set of acrylic nails and a rake of cheap costume jewellery on would leave his face like a busted sofa.'

In an even more brazen claim, however, 94 per cent of the women we surveyed felt they'd batter his opponent Scott Quigg with one arm tied behind their back.

'FFS, I've shit bigger than him,' said Gillian Uncooth today outside Primark. 'He looks like one of them scrawny reduced price chickens ye get in Tesco before closing time. Not a pick of meat on him. A good boot in the balls and he'd be away crying to his ma.

'Frampton should win,' she continued, 'but I reckon I'd beat him too. I mean they're two grown men fighting over a PURSE for feck sake! F**king lightweights.'

'Actually they're bantamweights,' corrected her husband.

One hundred per cent of the men we surveyed thought that all the women we surveyed were talking out of their holes.

NI paramilitaries threaten new terror campaign over EU status

Following the UK's vote to leave the EU, The Ulster Fry has learned that Northern Ireland paramilitaries are set to take up arms again to fight for the opposing sides.

We understand that the IRA Army Council met yesterday at an undisclosed location that Gerry Adams denies ever visiting. After again failing to find a solution for the longstanding problem of 'IRA Army Council' having the word 'army' in it twice, they eventually agreed on a new bombing and terror campaign.

'We're gonna resume bombing England next month,' confirmed Fiachra O'Fuchstiych from the Irish Republican Army Army Council. 'We think it's a disgrace that Britain wants its independence, so our campaign of terror won't stop until we achieve a full twenty-eight country united Europe.'

Loyalists meanwhile have taken the opposing view and want to celebrate the break from their oppressive European overlords.

'For too long now we were patronised with billions of euros of European peace funding money to regenerate our towns and cities,' declared Donna Sashmore from UDA continuity group, UDB. 'We plan on reclaiming our communities and restoring them to their former glory by carrying out target bombing attacks across East Belfast.'

An early security alert was reported near Albertbridge Road this morning after a cavalcade of PSNI Land Rovers was seen converging on a desolate business area left ravaged by vicious attacks. However it was later revealed just to have been police officers going for an early lunch at KFC in Connswater.

Boris Johnson, meanwhile, has revealed one of the reasons why he seemed to shy away from the Brexit team once victory was won. 'I could handle being on the same side as nutters like George Galloway and Nigel Farage,' said the tousle-haired Tory, 'but Sammy Wilson was a step too far.'

> The IRA Army Council met yesterday at an undisclosed location that Gerry Adams denies ever visiting.

Local baby sets new world record for socks retention

A nine-month-old baby from County Down has stunned experts at the Guinness Book of Records by successfully keeping both of his socks on for a half-hour period.

Tom McWilliams, a self-employed fart generator from Dundonald, set the new world record during a car journey into the city centre. It is understood that he maintained his pairing the entire way to Knock, before losing control of his left sock in Ballyhackamore.

'It's a miraculous achievement,' says Guinness adjudicator Ross McNorris. 'We've never seen such astounding sock control from an infant. This bodes well for the Northern Ireland team in the 2016 Rio Baby Olympics.'

This is just the latest in a series of successful baby-related record attempts by local youngsters. In February 12-month-old Lucas Flange from Bangor managed to keep a dummy in his mouth for seventy-five seconds before spitting it into a puddle, and just last week two-year-old Dungannon girl Hermione Donaghy astonished experts by waking up facing the same direction as she went to sleep in three nights in a row.

However, the news has not been universally welcomed. Ten-month old Jack Flack, Chair of the Confederation of Baby Industries, has hit out at what he describes as 'unashamed Babysploitation' and 'a betrayal of the basic principles of infanthood'.

'Everyone knows that babies lose socks as a method of adult control,' he told us. 'Bigger people can't resist baby feet, so random shedding of footwear is essential if we are to maintain our dominion over them. This type of blatant publicity-seeking will only encourage other kids to keep their socks on, and it must be nipped in the bud by all right-thinking toddlers.'

The record breaker himself was unavailable for comment, as he was too busy eating the discarded sock.

> Tom McWilliams, a self-employed fart generator from Dundonald, set the record during a car journey into the city centre, maintaining his pairing as far as Knock.

Index of Ulster place names

Abbey Centre 87, 106
Aldergrove 18
Antrim 13, 20. 32, 33, 47, 63, 83, 88, 91, 106, 113, 114, 120, 125
Antrim Road Waterworks 82
Ardoyne 15, 57
Ards Peninsula 114
Ards Shopping Centre 100, 114
Armagh 36, 72, 104, 122
Aughnacloy 72, 117

Balix 88
Ballyclare 111
Ballyhackamore 127
Ballyhalbert 71, 114
Ballylumford 60, 126
Ballymena 15, 95, 103, 120
Ballymoney 88, 120
Ballywalter 16, 22
Banbridge 17, 111
Bangor 42, 46, 60, 70, 127
Belfast 11, 12, 14, 15, 16, 18, 20, 23, 24, 26, 28, 31, 37, 41, 43, 46, 50, 52, 56, 57, 60, 61, 62, 64, 65, 71, 72, 74, 81, 83, 87, 88, 93, 95, 96, 101, 102, 103, 106, 110, 111, 112, 115, 119, 120, 121, 122, 123, 126
East Belfast 28, 41, 63, 124
North Belfast 15, 33, 56, 57
South Belfast 110
West Belfast 31, 37, 115, 126
Belfast Central Station 119
Bogside 95

Carnlough 125
Carrickfergus 55, 88, 125
Castlecourt 26, 110, 121
Castledawson 12
Claudy 12

Connswater 124
Cookstown 10, 40, 72
Corbet 17
Craigadick 88
Craigavon 18, 49, 50, 51, 66, 81, 90, 104, 107
Cranfield 90
Crawfordsburn 53
Creggan 26, 42

Derry see Londonderry
Doagh 125
Donegal 30, 88
Donemanagh 71, 88
Dromore 50
Dundonald 40, 90, 96, 127
Dungannon 95, 117, 127
Dungiven 36, 62, 104
Dunmurry 115

Eglinton 88
Enniskillen 77

Fermanagh 29, 55, 59, 72
Foyle 28

Giant's Ring 88
Glenavon 18
Glengormley 93
Glenshane Mountains 84
Glenshane Pass 63, 104, 126

Havelock House 96, 116
Hillsborough 31, 42, 50, 53, 93
Holywood 31, 42, 53, 102

Kilkeel 72
Knock 127

Larne 12, 33, 47, 91, 102, 114, 116
Limavady 12, 32
Lisburn 27, 32, 43, 48, 50, 111
Lisnaskea 71

Londonderry see Derry
Lough Neagh 26
Lower Ballinderry 120
Lurgan 18, 40, 42, 47, 48, 50, 76, 104

Maghera 88
Magherafelt 36, 60
Muff 88

Newry 36, 72, 76, 93
Newtownabbey 106
Newtownards 44, 100, 114
Nutts Corner Market 83

Omagh 25, 40, 113

Plumbridge 88
Portadown 18, 30
Portavogie 120
Portrush 63, 67, 88, 90
Portstewart 67

Rathcoole 42, 87, 90, 106
Rathfriland 50
Ringsend 88
Rostrevor 72

Scarva 55
Slieve Donard 26, 42
Sprucefield 111
Stormont 17, 18, 26, 28, 33, 34, 35, 41, 50, 113, 125
Strabane 27, 49, 58, 62, 70, 107, 110, 113, 116
Stranagalwilly 88

Tullycarnet 27
Twinbrook 96
Tyrone 14, 25, 27, 72, 88, 113, 116, 120

Upper Ballinderry 120